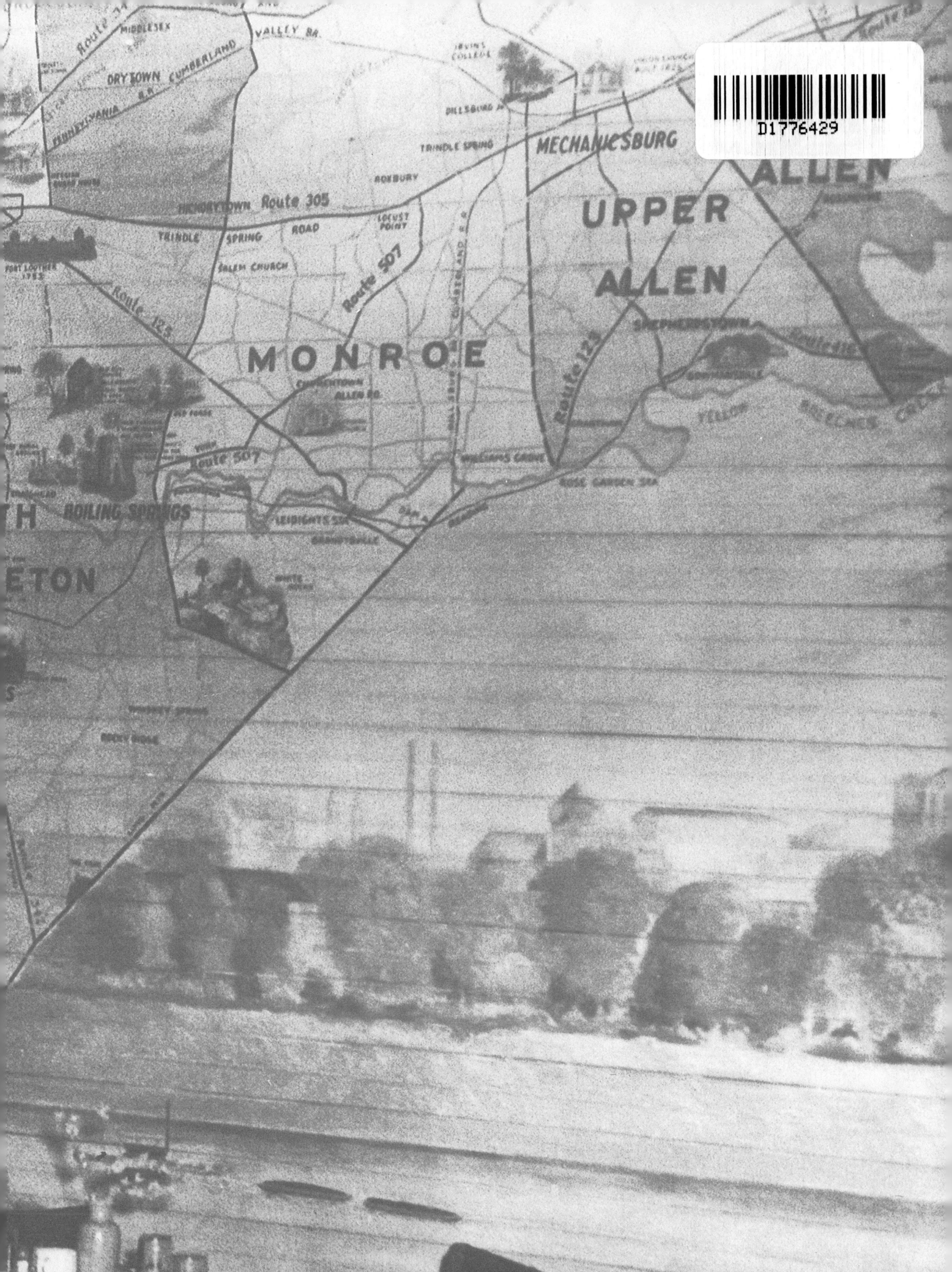

Past Receipts
Present Recipes

Past Receipts Present Recipes

Presented by the
Cumberland County
Historical Society

First Edition
First Printing, September 1996
3,000

(c) Copyright 1996, Cumberland County Historical Society

All rights reserved.

1996 edition limited to 3000 copies

ISBN : 0 - 9638923 - 3 - 9

Additional copies may be obtained by writing :

Cumberland County Historical Society
and The Hamilton Library Association
21 North Pitt Street
Carlisle, Pennsylvania 17013
(717) 249-7610

Please enclose $35.00, plus $4.00 postage and handling and 6% sales tax, PA residents only.

``Throughout this book CCHS is the abbreviation of the Cumberland County Historical Society.''

Book design by Susan D'Lamater.

Printed by Repro Graphics, Lewisberry Pennsylvania

Bookcover, Dickinson College Eating Club, Carlisle, c. 1910

Inside bookcover, Bosler Room, Fairfield Hall, Allenberry, Boiling Springs, painted in 1934 by Paul A. Bloser.

This book is dedicated to husbands, children and friends
who sacrificed waistlines and time for our book.
We are truly grateful to
Oliver Hazan,
co-owner and chef of
The California Cafe, Carlisle,
whose expertise was always available
and whose wit was always appreciated.

Cookbook Committee

Chair

MARY PAT WENTZEL

Editors

ANN KRAMER HOFFER

ANDREA SHEYA

MARY PAT WENTZEL

SUSAN D'LAMATER

SONDRA ELIAS

GRETCHEN HOFFMAN

VIRGINIA A. LaFOND

JACKIE MARTIN

PATTI OWEN

ANNE PASS

MAUREEN REED

JEAN SOREM

PAT STRICKLER

EILEEN SWIDLER

VIRGINIA WENTZEL

CONTENTS

8	PEACHY PARKER, THE INSPIRATION
10	THE PAST AND THE PRESENT
14	HORS D' OEUVRES
48	SOUPS
72	SALADS
106	ENTREES
158	VEGETABLES AND SIDE DISHES
184	SAUCES AND ACCOMPANIMENTS
200	BREAKFAST
218	BREADS
234	DESSERTS
286	THE SOCIETY TODAY
288	ACKNOWLEDGEMENTS
291	INDEX

Peachy Parker

Foreward

In no sense must this be considered a "Complete Cook Book." Indeed I never but one that claimed to this destruction. I discovered it among a lot of old books in the attic when as a girl of sixteen my interest in things Culinary was first aroused. Evidently the book had been presented to my Grand Mother whose keen sense of humor had induced her to preserve and pin to it the accompanying note

"My dear Mrs P.
    I send you these old Cookery books of ___ I do not consider them of any value. I found them among some old papers in the library. They will be probably of no use to you & with me they are and were thrown a-side.
    Yours."

Patriotic Creams.

American Cream.

½ box of gelatine.
½ pt. of milk.
1 cup of sugar.
Juice and rind of one lemon.
Cover the gelatine with a half cup of cold water and soak half an hour. Put the milk on to boil in a farina boiler, add the gelatine to it, stir until dissolved. Strain and take from the fire and stand aside until cool. When cold add the sugar and lemon, stir well, turn into a mould and stand away to harden. Serve with cream or Vanilla sauce. This will serve eight persons.

The Inspiration

The imposing red brick Greek Revival Style house standing at 141 West High Street in Carlisle has a history all of its own. Who would have thought that its resident, Miss Peachy Parker, would have been the inspiration for this project.

By 1910, Emeline Knox Parker (Miss Peachy) had compiled a cookbook of her own. Its title was "A Little Book of Excellent Recipes from Colonial Times to the Present." Early recipes were also referred to as receipts. Volunteers at the Society discovered this book. Their fascination with the cookbook and the efforts of Martha Wilson to type the collection persuaded all that the Society should compile its own book by 1996.

Today Boyer and Ritter CPA has offices in the Parker House. But by 1900, Miss Peachy was the third generation of the Parker Family to live in this grand house. Issac Brown Parker, a prospering lawyer, originally bought the house in 1813. His wife remodeled and rebuilt the house adding the imposing facade and doorway, plaster rosettes on the ceiling and the curving stairway inside. It was in this ambience that Miss Peachy lived. Her book tries to capture the past and present as people around her remember it. Her enthusiasm encouraged us to do the same.

A.K.H.

The Past and the Present

The finest food and drink, the most refined customs for their consumption, and exquisite or charming equipment for their service all comprise the human experience of nourishment. *Tradition*, *ceremony*, even *ritual* are as important to the psyche as food is to the body. As far back as archaeology can take us into the lives of our ancestors, we find that the gratification provided by food and drink has also implied traditional methods of preparation, ceremonial presentation, and life-affirming rituals. Our world may abound with fast-food, microwave ovens, plastic and paper containers, yet more cookbooks and "life-style" magazines are coming off the presses now than all those which were previously published put together! While some food professionals struggle to come up with ways to prepare food faster and more uniformly, other chefs, caterers, and home-makers imaginatively create ever more subtle and complex fare.

Children, especially, crave the tradition and ceremony of food. What toddler has not refused to drink except out of his own special cup or disdained to eat his vegetables until after the meat is finished? Children, and the child in each of us, often are offended by changes in menus or recipes for festive favorites; if a chocolate birthday cake was presented last year, a chocolate cake is anticipated this year. Thanksgiving dinner without a roasted turkey is unimaginable! Styles of cooking come and go, but the most traditional foods—soups, stews, breads—maintain their evocative resonance for both body and spirit. Even thinking about such sustenance brings reassurance in our hectic world. I find myself being nurtured just by reading recipes for wonderful food at the same time I send my kids for take-out pizza when I arrive home too tired to cook!

While we yearn for continuity and comfort, we also always have craved the novel and exotic in our diet. We learn early in school that the European exploration of the Far East and the New World was driven by a rage for new and different foods, beverages, and flavorings. No one would buy cookbooks if new ways of preparing food were not desirable; but as we develop a universal culture, history is perhaps the last frontier we can explore in our search of something different.

Indeed, there is much we can learn from the past to fulfill our aspirations for lives of grace and meaning. Why not revert to the eighteenth-century custom of inviting friends to an "entertainment" rather than the well-worn "party"? Our ancestors assembled with the unspoken understanding that a guest was as responsible for the success of a social event as the host. Each guest came prepared to contribute congenial conversation, graceful accomplishments in music and dancing, or at least an attractive if not decorative appearance instead of being a mere passive consumer. In

Turkey Dinner, Cumberland County, c. 1920, -CCHS

other words, a guest expected to entertain rather than to be entertained—isn't that "attitude adjustment" at its best? Not that all of our ancestors frowned on enhancing an occasion with fortified beverages! Punch made of rum or other spirits, sugar, and citrus fruits differed only in name from daiquiris, whiskey sours, or old fashioneds; and ever ready, over-flowing punch bowls oiled the wheels of masculine hospitality and conviviality.

Bounty was a word our forefathers thoroughly understood. Ironically, with the increased availability of different foods, menus have diminished rather than expanded. Variety of choice instead of quantity of any single food was the axiom of the past when several meats, fowls, and fishes prepared in different ways and accompanied by numerous vegetables were served at every meal. In this day of dinner tables laid with one casserole, a salad, some bread, and a "lite" dessert, hostesses may find that reverting to greater variety solves the growing problems of guest's allergies and special diets.

A Moore Family Picnic, Two Mile House, South Middleton Township, c. 1930, -CCHS, Moore Collection

Just a few years ago, I was shocked to overhear a middle-aged guest complain at being asked to pour tea at a lovely and traditional party; "teas" had become so rare that women themselves forgot that only the most honored or socially senior ladies "poured." This custom harks back to the early eighteenth century when tea was too expensive to be entrusted to servants, and only the mistress of the house kept the key and measured out the precious herb. The extravagant value of tea provided Western women with their first acceptable and recognized role in social life. The essential, imported porcelain teapots and cups also were too fragile and rare to be touched by scullery maids so the lady of the house herself washed them, often in the drawing room, and dried them with the finest linen "tea towel". Happily, tea and its accompanying delicacies are again in fashion as women who have battled the "glass-ceilings" of business and academia rediscover the pleasures of female companionship.

At the same time that recipes and bizarre ingredients are proliferating, store shelves and household cupboards never before have been so stuffed with attractive, attainable, and distinctive dishes, glassware, and other food service items. Many young people are even rediscovering the joys of caring for and using the fine linens and silver which their mothers once gratefully discarded in favor of permanent-press placemats and stainless steel spoons. We may be amused by the bourgeois pretensions of late-Victorian Americans who demanded a different fork or spoon for every imaginable morsel from sardines and mangos to *petits fours* and peas, but we revel in the charm of discovering such exotica and finding ways of putting them back to use with foods we otherwise might not prepare.

We bond with the past when we recognize that some of the things we think most contemporary are merely reiterations of history. The most fashionable silver pitchers made four-hundred years ago during the reign of Elizabeth I replicated wooden barrels complete with chased grain and knots; two hundred years later early American silversmiths copied the same "conceit" of rustic objects mimicked in silver by making "hooped" or barrel-like tankards of the precious metal. A hundred years ago, silver nut dishes were formed as bark-covered hollow logs, and today Tiffany sells silver imitation stapled-slat strawberry baskets. Bridal headpieces descend directly from the fresh floral crowns awarded medieval guests, and birthday party "goodie bags" six-hundred years ago were small baskets of sweetmeats presented to guests so that they might prolong and savor the pleasures of a feast. Even the avant-garde vogue for flavoring main dishes with unusual spices, herbs, and sweet fruits is but a return to the cooking styles of the Middle Ages and Renaissance which relied on orange water, saffron, and even cinnamon and chocolate for flavoring meats.

Dining with delectation and style has always been a balance between the tried-and-true and the new-and-novel. In this book I hope you will find some of both and perhaps be inspired to continue exploring the past as well as the present to create the traditions of the future.

Jennifer F. Goldsborough

Jennifer Faulds Goldsborough, a consulting curator to the Maryland Historical Society, became a friend of the Society's when she was a lecturer at the 1995 Antiques Forum. Her enthusiasm for the many aspects of the dining experience matched her extensive knowledge.

HORS D'OEUVRES

Almond Cheese Strips

Serves Six to Eight

A *marvelous make ahead.*

- 6 slices of cooked bacon, crumbled
- 1 3 ounce package sliced almonds, chopped
- 2 teaspoons Worcestershire sauce
- ½ pound sharp cheddar cheese, shredded
- 1 cup mayonnaise
- salt and pepper to taste
- 1 loaf thin-sliced white bread (crusts removed)

Combine all ingredients except bread. Spread mixture on bread slices. Cut into strips, place on cookie sheets, and freeze. Once frozen, store in plastic bags in freezer. When needed, remove from bags, place on cookie sheets and bake at 400° for 10 minutes.

Wilma B. Prescott

Note
Do not omit freezing step.

Baked Cheese Dip

Serves Eight to Ten

C *ocktail party pleaser.*

- 4 cups grated sharp Cheddar cheese
- 1 cup grated mozzarella cheese
- 2 cups mayonnaise
- 1 small onion to taste
- 1 dash of Worcestershire sauce
- 1 round loaf pumpernickel bread

Preheat oven to 350°. Mix together all ingredients. Place in hollowed out pumpernickel bread. Place foil around the edges and bake 20 to 30 minutes. Top with bacon bits and bake 10 minutes more.

Serve with cubed bread or crackers.

Virginia Wentzel

Overleaf, **James Redmond, Butler**
Two Mile House
South Middleton Township
c. 1920

-CCHS, Moore Collection

16 PAST RECEIPTS PRESENT RECIPES

Hot Pecan Pie

Serves Twelve

Valuable addition to your recipe files—perfect for any party.

Preheat oven to 350°. Thin the sour cream with milk. Add cream cheese, dried beef, onions and pepper. Place in a 8 inch pyrex pie plate. Brown pecans in butter and spread on top. Bake for 15 minutes. Serve hot with crackers.

Jackie Martin

- ½ cup sour cream
- 2 tablespoons milk
- 8 ounces cream cheese, softened
- 1 2 ½ ounce package dried beef, cut fine
- 2 tablespoons finely chopped onions
- ½ teaspoon pepper

For the topping
- ¼ cup pecans, chopped
- 2 tablespoons butter

Monte Carlo Spread

Serves Twelve

Try stuffing celery, pea pods or Belgian endive with this spread.

Blend cream cheese and anchovy paste. Add capers, chill. Serve on crackers or toast.

Elizabeth Hean Stone

- 2 8 ounce packages cream cheese
- 1 tube anchovy paste
- 1 heaping tablespoon drained, minced capers

Olive Nut Spread

Serves Six to Eight

So good you won't believe the ingredients.

- 3 ounces cream cheese, softened
- ½ cup walnuts, finely chopped
- ¼ cup green pimento stuffed olives, finely chopped
- 2 tablespoons milk
- Pepperidge Farm thin sliced white bread
- olive slices for garnish

Mix all ingredients by hand. Trim crusts from bread. Spread bread with cheese mixture, and cut into three pieces. Garnish with olive slices.

Holly Tiley

18 PAST RECEIPTS PRESENT RECIPES

Pecan Cheese Log

Makes Two Rolls

This makes a delicious holiday or hostess gift.

Blend all ingredients except paprika and some of the pecans. Shape into 2 rolls about 7"x1½" and wrap in aluminum foil. Chill thoroughly -- overnight if possible. When chilled, roll in remaining pecans and paprika. Serve roll with Triscuits or slice and serve on crackers. Roll may be kept frozen and used as needed over a period of time.

Mary Thomas Reed

- 2 cups chopped pecans
- 1 small clove garlic, mashed
- 11 ounces cream cheese
- 5 ounces Bleu cheese
- ½ teaspoon Worcestershire sauce
- ½ teaspoon salt
- ¼ teaspoon hot pepper sauce or Tabasco
- 2 tablespoons paprika

At left, **A & P Store**
5-7 South Hanover Street
Carlisle
c. 1945

-CCHS

At far left, **Mentzer College Girls in Garden**
North Hanover Street
Carlisle
c. 1912
A. A. Line, Photographer

-CCHS

MOLDED CRAB SPREAD

Serves Twelve

This is sure to be a favorite with your guests.

1   envelope unflavored gelatin
1   can cream of mushroom soup
6   ounces cream cheese, softened
1   cup mayonnaise or salad dressing
1½ cups chopped celery
1   small onion, chopped fine
1   pound fresh crab meat, hard particles removed

Soften gelatin in 3 tablespoons water. Heat soup and gelatin together. Add cream cheese, mayonnaise, celery, onion and crab meat. Pour into large mold greased with vegetable oil. Refrigerate over night before serving. Loosen mold by setting it in hot water before inverting. Serve with crackers of choice.

Helen Ashway

CRAB DIP

Serves Eight to Twelve

Easy but with a gourmet appeal.

24 ounces cream cheese (preferably whipped)
2   tablespoons chopped onion
2   tablespoons horseradish
1   tablespoon milk
1   pound lump crab meat
    almonds

Preheat oven to 375°. Mix the first four ingredients until soft and well blended. Add crab. Place in baking dish. Sprinkle with almonds. Bake until bubbly. Let cool slightly. Serve with crackers or french bread.

Frances Del Duca

Old Bar
Boiling Springs Hotel
now Boiling Springs Tavern
c. 1908

-CCHS

Green Vegetable Dip

Serves Twelve

An hors d'oeuvre with little fuss.

- 1 regular sized box of frozen spinach
- ½ cup chopped fresh parsley
- 1 teaspoon salt
- ½-1 teaspoon ground black pepper
- ½ cup chives, finely chopped (or green onions)
- 2 cups mayonnaise

Combine spinach, which has been thawed, drained and squeezed until nearly dry with remaining ingredients. Mix thoroughly. Cover and refrigerate. Will keep several days in the refrigerator.

Emmy Robbins Stuart

Note

This is best if made one day before serving.

Chicken Canapes

Serves Twenty

These amazingly good and addictive canapes were introduced to Carlisle by the wife of a former Dean of the Dickinson School of Law.

- **Pepperidge Farm Bread**
- 2 quarts (8 c) chopped cooked chicken
- 1 cup finely chopped celery
- 1 cup chopped pecans or chestnuts
- 1 cup mayonnaise (or more)
- 2 tablespoons seasoned salt
- ½ teaspoon curry (mild)
- 2 tablespoon lemon juice
- ½ cup finely chopped or grated onion
- 1 4 ounce jar pimento strips for decoration
- 2 cups grated sharp cheese, optional

Mix ingredients until well blended. Spread on buttered whole wheat (or white) Pepperidge Farm bread. Cut off crusts, and cut into rectangles or squares. Chicken spread can be made one day ahead and refrigerated. Spread may be put on bread and refrigerated a few hours before serving.

Ann King

Low Cal Dip

Serves Six

Light and low in fat, but satisfying in flavor.

Peel and seed cucumbers, grind remaining portion. Wrap ground cucumber in paper towels to remove excess moisture. Drain shrimp. Mix all ingredients together. Serve with sturdy crackers.

Sue Reed

2 to 3 cucumbers
1 cup cottage cheese
1 small can of shrimp
1 tablespoon horseradish

Menu Cover
Julius Restaurant
49 West Main Street
Carlisle
1930

-CCHS

HORS D'OEUVRES 25

Milk Wagon
George W. Shughart
Carlisle
c. 1898

-CCHS, Gift of Mrs. Blanche Ebener

Chicken Satay

Serves Eight

You may want to serve this as a main course.

Combine first three ingredients. Pour over chicken, cover and refrigerate overnight, turning occasionally. Soak bamboo skewers at least 1 hour in warm water and skewer chicken lengthwise. Discard marinade. Broil, watching carefully, turning after several minutes until golden brown. Preparation time: 10 minutes Cooking time: 5-10 minutes

- 1 package Thai peanut sauce for Satay
- 1/2 can coconut milk
- 1 tablespoon soy sauce
- 1 package chicken tenders or 2 breasts cut into 1" x 4" strips
- 1 package short bamboo skewers

Susan Watchorn

Note
A favorite among lovers of Thai cuisine. Serve with Peanut Sauce.

Peanut Sauce

Yields One and One-half Cups

This sauce may also be used with pork satay.

Heat milk; add curry paste, stirring to blend. Add peanut butter. Stir until smooth. Add sugar, continuing to stir. Let set. Serve warm. Preparation time: 10 minutes Cooking time: 10 minutes Should be prepared just prior to serving, but can be prepared several hours ahead, chilled and reheated, stirring frequently.

- 1/2 can coconut milk
- 1/3 tin curry paste
- 12 ounces peanut butter
- 2 1/2 teaspoons sugar

Susan Watchorn

Hawaiian Sea Anemones

Makes One Dozen

Enjoy these with duck sauce, soy sauce or hot mustard.

- ½ pound raw shrimp, shelled and finely chopped
- 2 tablespoons scallions, finely chopped
- 3 or 4 water chestnuts, chopped
- 1 teaspoon sherry
- 1 teaspoon salt
- 1½ teaspoons cornstarch
- ¼ bunch oriental vermicelli (bean thread or cellophane noodles) cut into one inch lengths (soak in water for 20 minutes before using).
- 2 cups vegetable oil for frying

Combine first six ingredients. Shape into one dozen round balls. Roll balls into cut vermicelli, pressing lightly until covered. Deep fry in hot oil. The vermicelli will puff up, turn white and crisp when cooked. To prepare ahead: In the morning, make shrimp balls, roll in vermicelli. Cover with foil and refrigerate. Fry just before serving.

Carol Green

Note

The fat must be hot enough to fry the noodles quickly: you can drop in a few strands to test. I usually use a Crisco type shortening; peanut oil is lighter and more delicate but more expensive. The shrimp balls float to the top of the fat and must be turned over to cook on both sides. These are at their best when cooked just before serving.

Kramer's Corner
West High Street at Courthouse Alley
Carlisle
c. 1900

-CCHS

Liver Paté

Makes Three Cups

Always a welcome addition to a cocktail party.

- 1½ pounds chicken livers
- ¼ cup bacon fat (or 3 tablespoons)
- 1 medium onion chopped
- 2 whole cloves
- 1 bay leaf
- nutmeg
- salt
- coarse pepper
- 3 tablespoons white wine
- 6 tablespoons butter
- crackers, bread

Bake first five ingredients in covered casserole at 350° for 1 hour. Add to taste, seasonings and wine. Place in blender with butter. Grind to form a smooth pate. Place in earthenware container and refrigerate.

Martha Martin

Below, **The Carlisle Inn**
*800 North Hanover Street
Carlisle
c. 1935*

-Charles A. B. Heinze Collection

30 PAST RECEIPTS PRESENT RECIPES

The CARLISLE INN

ON UNITED STATES ROUTE NUMBER ELEVEN · CARLISLE · PENNA ·

PASTRY SNAILS

Roll into very thin oblongs

    Pie Crust
Spread the oblongs with filling

Roll them like a jelly roll chill the rolls, cut them into 1/2 inch slices and bake them on a greased pan in a hot oven   425*

Fillings:

    Grated American Cheese seasoned with Cayenne.

    Soft cream cheese seasoned with salt and paprika

    Braunschweiger sausage thinned with tomato soup seasoned with worcestershire sauce.

                  Mrs/ Williams

Black Bean Olé

Serves Eight to Ten

Adds a south of the border touch to a party.

- 1 can refried beans (fat free optional)
- ⅓ cup mild onion, chopped
- ⅓ cup sour cream (fat fee optional)
- 1¼ cups Cheddar cheese, grated - save ½ cup cheese for topping
- 4 tablespoons chopped jalapeño pepper, optional
- 2 15 ounce cans of black beans, drained

Preheat oven to 350°. Mix all ingredients together. Place in 9x13 dish. Top with remaining cheese. Bake for 25 minutes or until bubbly.

Patti Owen

Black Bean Hummus

Serves Eight to Ten

Hummus with a Southwestern twist.

- 2 cups canned black beans (19 oz. can), drained and rinsed
- 1 cup canned chick peas (½ of a 19 oz. can) drained and rinsed
- 1 head of garlic
  olive oil to drizzle
- 1 teaspoon ground cumin
- 1 tablespoon tahini sauce
  juice of 2 lemons
- ¼ cup olive oil

In a 375° oven, roast garlic head with olive oil drizzled on it for 1 hour. After cooling, slip cloves out of skin and place in food processor. Add 1¼ cup of black beans, chick peas, cumin, tahini, lemon juice and ¼ cup of olive oil. After pureed, add remaining ¼ cup of black beans to dip. May be made up to 3 days ahead.

Andrea Sheya

Bar-B-Q Meatballs

Serves Six

Good as a main dish, too.

TO MAKE THE SAUCE
Heat ketchup, brown sugar and Worcestershire sauce.

TO MAKE THE MEATBALLS
Preheat oven to 350°. Mix ground meat, evaporated milk, Worcestershire , and dry soup mix. Allow mixture to set. Make into small meatballs. Place in 9 x 13" pan. Bake for 15 to 20 minutes, until brown. Drain well and put into sauce.

Dolly Scholl

Note
May be prepared ahead and frozen. Thaw and heat to serve.

For the Sauce
- 2 cups ketchup
- 1 cup brown sugar
- 2 tablespoons Worcestershire sauce

For the Meatballs
- 1½ pounds ground meat
- ⅔ cup evaporated milk
- 2 teaspoons Worcestershire sauce
- 2 packages dried Lipton onion soup mix

White Linament

1/2 pint turpentine   1/2 pint vinegar
4 eggs   8 ounces household ammonia

Beat eggs and add vinegar, a little at a time. Keep beating and add turpentine slowly. Keep beating and add ammonia slowly. After all is well mixed, place in tight jar and shake. The more you shake, the better the results. It will be dark at first. The more you shake, the lighter it will get until it turns white. Rub on skin for aches and pains. Works on horses too.

Deborah K. Westbrook

Cucumber Sandwiches

Serves Ten to Twelve

 *nice accompaniment with afternoon tea.*

2 English cucumbers (long, wrapped in cellophane)
1 loaf Pepperidge Farm thin sliced bread, white or wheat
butter
salt
pepper
fresh dill

Thinly slice 2 English cucumbers. Put in a bowl and sprinkle with salt. Let stand 5 hours or overnight. Blot off excess moisture. Cut the crusts off the bread. Butter and layer cucumber slices on top. Dust with pepper and fresh dill. This is a closed sandwich. Cut into quarters.

Elizabeth Rousek

Watercress Sandwiches

Serves Ten to Twelve

 *popular Antiques Forum hors d'oeuvre with watercress from the LeTort Spring Run.*

1 bunch watercress
8 ounces cream cheese
mayonnaise (enough to make cream cheese spreadable)
1 loaf Pepperidge Farm bread

Wash and cut watercress. Discard stems. Cream watercress and a small amount of cream cheese together. Add a little mayonnaise. Spread on bread.

Mary Kramer

Chocolate Shop Sandwich Filling
Serves Eight

The Chocolate Shop was on West High Street and run by the Misses Mary Line and Mary Wetzel. It was the gathering place for Dickinson College students in the 1930's and 1940's. This is the sandwich filling they made famous.

Melt butter in saucepan; add dried beef and sauté very lightly. Add tomato soup. Beat egg, add to mixture. Add cheese. Bring to boil for one minute or longer to thicken. Store in glass jar in refrigerator.

Bea Williams, Margaret MacGregor, Hilda Arnold

- ¼ pound dried beef (chopped in food processor)
- ¼ pound sharp Cheddar cheese (chopped in food processor)
- 1 can tomato soup
- 1 egg
- 1 tablespoon butter

Cocktail Cheese Sandwiches
Serves Ten

Another Chocolate Shop favorite.

Grind sharp cheese, green pepper and a little onion. Cream together with a small amount of mayonnaise. Make into bite size sandwiches.

Ann Kramer Hoffer

- 1 cup grated white sharp cheese
- ½ cup chopped green pepper
- ¼ cup chopped onions
- mayonnaise
- Pepperidge Farm bread

HORS D'OEUVRES

CROSTINI CAPONATA

Serves Six to Twelve

Caponata is a wonderful side dish with grilled or roasted meats.

- 12 slices Italian bread, cut ½ inch thick
- ½ cup olive oil
- 1 eggplant at least 8 ounces
- 2 teaspoons salt
- ½ cup minced onion
- ½ cup minced celery
- ½ cup green pepper, minced
- 2 tablespoons fresh parsley
- ½ cup water
- ¼ cup tomato puree
- 6-8 pimento stuffed green olives
- 2 tablespoons capers, rinsed and drained
- ¼ teaspoon freshly grated pepper
- 1 tablespoon red wine vinegar
- 3 plum tomatoes, sliced

Preheat oven to 350°. Brush both sides of bread with olive oil. Place in baking sheet. Bake 5 minutes on each side or until lightly toasted. Cut eggplant into ½ inch slices. Place in colander and sprinkle with salt. Place on a plate with weight on top, and drain for 1 hour. Pat eggplant dry with paper towels. In a large frying pan, heat ¼ cup olive oil over medium heat. Add onions and cook 3 to 4 minutes until softened. Stir in celery and pepper, and cook 3 to 4 minutes longer. Stir in eggplant, water and 1 tablespoon of the tomato puree. Cook, stirring frequently 3 minutes to blend flavors. Remove pan from heat and stir in vinegar. Let stand 30 to 60 minutes. Pile caponata on crostini and garnish with tomatoes, capers and parsley.

Judy Castrina

MARINATED BRUSSELS SPROUTS

Serves Eight to Ten

Brussels sprouts have never tasted so good.

- 3 packages frozen Brussels sprouts
- ½ to ⅝ cup Italian salad dressing
- ½ teaspoon dill weed
- 1 tablespoon minced onion

Mix together Italian salad dressing, dill weed and onion. Cook Brussels sprouts as directed on package. Drain sprouts. Pour dressing mixture over hot sprouts, cover and marinate for 24 hours in refrigerator. Drain most of marinade off of sprouts when ready to serve. Serve with toothpicks. Keeps well in refrigerator for several days.

Emmy Robins Stuart

Minted Melon Balls

Serves Ten to Twelve

Cool, refreshing and colorful.

Make melon balls. Add liqueur and chill. Just before serving, add mint and serve with toothpicks.

Joyce Nelson

- 1 ripe honey dew
- 1 ripe cantaloupe
- ⅓ cup Grand Marnier liqueur
- ⅓ cup chopped fresh mint leaves

Carlisle Farmers Market
*York Road
Carlisle
1973*

-CCHS

Party Punch

Serves Twelve to Fifteen

Refreshing for the young and old.

- 1 large bottle grape juice
- 1 large container orange juice
- 1 large bottle gingerale
- ½ cup sugar
- 2 cups water
- 2 oranges, sliced thin and cut in half
- ice cubes

Blend the ingredients in a punch bowl.

Hilda Arnold

18th Century Tavern Mint Punch

Serves Twelve or More

This recipe is served at historic properties in Alexandria, Virginia.

- 1 cup finely chopped fresh mint leaves
- 1 6 ounce can lemonade concentrate, undiluted
- 1 64 ounce or 2–32 ounce bottles of gingerale
- ice cubes or ice ring

Mix lemonade, undiluted and mint leaves together. Add gingerale. Serve in 6 ounce cups and add 1 jigger of rum or bourbon per cup. As a time saver, mix lemonade and mint leaves together. Put into a plastic freezer bag and freeze. When ready to use, remove from freezer and add gingerale.

Emmy Robbins Stuart

Partytime
Carlisle Home
c. 1930

-CCHS

Mrs. Bosler's Champagne Punch

Serves Thirty to Thirty-five

This charming hostess enjoyed entertaining in her home on the corner of West High and College Streets.

- 5 quarts champagne
- 2 quarts brandy
- 16 oranges, squeezed
- 8 lemons, squeezed
- 1 pound sugar
- 1 pint water
- Canada Dry sparkling water

Make a simple syrup by stirring the sugar into the water until the sugar dissolves. Bring to boil and boil for three minutes. Store in a glass jar until ready to mix with the other ingredients.

Mary Wood Stuart

Antoinette's Sherry Punch

Serves Ten

Marvelous thirst quencher for the ladies.

- 1 6 ounce can of lemonade frozen concentrate
- 3 cans (lemonade can) cold water
- 3 cans (lemonade can) dry sherry

Combine in pitcher or punch bowl.

Lydia Hazlett

At right, **Tea at the McCreary home**
West King Street
Shippensburg
1896

-Shippensburg Historical Society Collection

PAST RECEIPTS PRESENT RECIPES

Egg Nog

Makes Two Quarts

Go ahead, splurge and enjoy.

- 12 eggs, separated
- 1 cup granulated sugar
- 4 cups brandy or rum
- 1 pint whipping cream

Beat yolks. Add sugar gradually until thick and brown colored. Add brandy or rum. Fold in whipped cream and beaten egg whites.

Catherine T. Scott

Grandma's Mint Julep

Serves One

Celebrate summer with this drink.

- 4 ounces bourbon per glass
- 4 top sprigs fresh mint per glass
- 1 teaspoon sugar per glass
- crushed ice to fill glass
- mint for garnish
- 1 12 ounce glass (chilled)

Wash the mint sprigs well, but do not shake. The night before serving (or in the morning), in a large mixing bowl, combine mint sprigs, sugar and bruise well with mallet or wooden spoon until it makes becomes very soft and sauce like. Pour bourbon over the mint mixture. Cover with a plate and let sleep. To serve, fill glass with crushed ice. Pour 4 ounces of julep in glass and garnish with a mint sprig. Serve with a straw.

George M. Saegmuller

Pink Ladies

Serves Eight

Be a health conscious hostess and substitute light cream.

Mix in a cocktail shaker and serve strained in stemmed glasses. (No ice in glasses).

Virginia A. LaFond

- 8 ounces apricot brandy
- 8 ounces grenadine
- 8 ounces gin
- 8 ounces heavy cream
- 5½ ounces lemon juice
- cracked ice (1 handful)

Wassail

Makes One Gallon

A bowl of Wassail is a Christmas Eve tradition for many families.

Mix fruit juices over low heat while adding sugar and spices. Do not use an iron pot. Add 5 cups hot water and 3 cups strong tea. Heat slowly on a low setting, about one hour. Do not let boil. Strain and discard spices. Just before serving, add brandy if desired.

Merri Lou Schaumann

- 6 ounce can frozen orange juice
- 6 ounce can frozen lemonade
- 1 quart apple juice
- ½ cup sugar
- ½ teaspoon whole cloves
- 2 sticks cinnamon
- 1 teaspoon ground ginger
- 5 cups hot water
- 3 cups strong tea
- 2 cups brandy, optional

BEVERAGES

Your Own Wine

Makes One Gallon

Try your hand at this easy method of wine making.

- 1 small can frozen grape juice concentrate
- 2 pounds granulated sugar
- 1 envelope dry yeast
- 1 gallon of water

Place ingredients into a gallon glass jug. Secure a balloon on a jug opening and let stand where temperature is between 72 and 80° for two months. Wine should be clarified and can be siphoned off. Only ¼ inch at the bottom will have to be discarded.

Mary Wheeler King

Tea Punch

Makes One Gallon

Iced tea with a punch.

- 7 tea bags
- 7 sprigs mint (3"-6" long)
- ¾ cup sugar or Sweet n' Low
- 1 6 ounce can frozen orange juice, thawed
- 1 6 ounce can frozen lemonade, thawed

Place tea bags, mint and sugar in a tea pot. Cover with boiling water and steep for at least 15 minutes. Strain into a one gallon container (a plastic milk jug works well). Add orange juice and lemonade. Fill container with water to make one gallon. This is best if made a day before using. It keeps several days in the refrigerator.

Mary Percival

At right, **Cloverdale Bottling Plant**
Newville
c. 1910
Maynard Hoover, photographer
-CCHS

Bloody Mary

Makes Eight Eight Ounce Drinks

Spice up the day with this recipe for Bloodies.

Mix and chill overnight first six ingredients. Stir in vodka. Sprinkle each drink with celery seed. If too hot, add 1 can of beef consommé.

Damien Elias

46	ounces tomato juice
¼	cup lemon juice
¼	cup Worcestershire sauce
1	teaspoon Tabasco
1½	teaspoons salt
1	teaspoon pepper
2	cups vodka
1	tablespoon celery seed

BEVERAGES

Soups

Creamed Corn Soup

Serves Four

When time is short, try this hearty soup.

- 2 cans of creamed corn
- 2 cans of milk (skim to whole)
- 2 tablespoons butter (optional)
- 1 tablespoons parsley (dried or fresh)
- 2 tablespoons chicken bouillon
- 1 package cheese tortellini

Empty 2 cans of creamed corn into a medium sized soup pot. Fill empty cans with milk and pour into the pot. Add butter, parsley and bouillon. Heat to boiling point, stirring occasionally. Add tortellini and bring to boil. Simmer for 8 to 10 minutes or until cheese tortellini are done, stirring occasionally.

Eileen Swidler

Molly Pitcher Hotel
*13 South Hanover Street
Carlisle
1944*

-CCHS

Overleaf, A. S. Hertzler Grocery Store
*West Coover and South Frederick Street
Mechanicsburg
c. 1910*

-Robert Rowe Collection

Chicken Corn Soup

Serves Eight To Ten

Serve this soup to out of town friends with homemade bread, apple butter and shoofly pie.

Cover cut up chicken with 3 quarts water. Stew until tender. Remove chicken from stock, strain stock and save. Pull meat from bones and cut into small pieces. Return chicken to stock; add potatoes, corn, noodles, parsley, eggs and salt and pepper. Cook until noodles and potatoes are done.

June Slep

- 1 4 to 5 pound chicken, cut into pieces
- 3 large potatoes, diced
- 2 boxes frozen corn or fresh cut from the cob
- 2 cups noodles
- 2 hard boiled eggs, chopped
- ¼ cup fresh parsley, salt and pepper to taste

Chicken Corn Noodle Soup

Serves Six

Easy to assemble with ingredients from cupboards and freezer.

Sauté onion in olive oil in a large pot. Add chicken breasts, broth, carrots, marjoram and thyme. Poach chicken for 20 minutes. Remove chicken, cut into bite-sized pieces, and return to pot. Add water and corn and cook for 30 minutes. Add parsley, noodles, and salt and pepper to taste. Cook 10 minutes or until noodles are done.

Greg Harder

- 1 medium onion, chopped
- 1 tablespoon olive oil
- 2 cans chicken broth (14½ ounces each)
- 1 pound skinless, boneless chicken breasts
- 4 carrots, sliced
- ¼ teaspoon marjoram
- ¼ teaspoon thyme
- 4 cups water
- 1 pound frozen corn
- ⅓ cup chopped parsley
- 6 ounces small egg noodles salt and pepper to taste

Oyster Stewpendous

Serves Four

Enjoy with Chesapeake Bay oysters.

- 1 cup milk
- 1 low salt chicken bouillon cube
- 1 cup diced potatoes
- 1 medium onion, diced
- ½ cup shredded carrots
- ½ cup diced celery
- 1 teaspoon salt
- 1 pint oysters
- 1 teaspoon curry powder
- 1 cup half and half or milk
- 4 ounces Monterey Jack cheese, cut in ½ inch cubes

In a 2½ quart saucepan simmer milk and bouillon. Add potatoes, onion, carrots, celery and salt. Simmer until vegetables are tender. Add oysters and simmer 10 minutes more. Mix curry powder and cream; add to vegetables. Simmer an additional 4 minutes to heat through. Divide cheese cubes evenly between 4 serving bowls and pour hot stew over the top.

Marcie Addams

Note

Add a dash of Tabasco sauce for added flavor.

Carlisle's Best Equipped Restaurant   Ladies' Private Entrance

QUICK LUNCH
E. I. SPAHR, Proprietor

Special Attention Given to Supplying the Family Trade with all Kinds of Sea Foods, Flaked Crab Meats Our Specialty. Oysters Supplied During the Summer. A Large Finely Equipped Dining Room on the Second Floor   -o-   -o-   -o-   -o-   -o-

121 W. HIGH STREET   CARLISLE, PA.

Quick Lunch Oyster Bar
121 West High Sreet
Carlisle
c. 1917

-CCHS, Griffith Collection

Scallop Chowder

Serves Six

From Cape Cod to Cumberland County—good and easy.

- 2 potatoes, boiled, peeled and chopped into bite sized pieces
- 2 onions, chopped
- 4 tablespoons butter, divided
- 2 cups milk
- 1½ cups light cream
- 1 pound bay scallops
- 1 pound frozen corn, cooked (or canned corn)
- chives or bacon to garnish

Simmer onions in 2 tablespoons butter until tender. Add 2 tablespoons of butter and sauté scallops just until they are cooked through, about 5 minutes. In a saucepan, heat milk and cream, potatoes and corn. Heat through, but do not boil. Add scallops and onion mixture. Serve with chives or crumbled bacon on top.

Carol Ferenz

-CCHS, **Postcard Collection**
1910

Tuna Cheese Chowder

Serves Four to Six

This soup may be made with cooked chicken. You may also substitute one half cup chopped, sautéd celery in place of the celery seed.

Sauté onions and carrots in butter until soft but not brown. Blend in flour. Add milk and broth. Cook and stir until thickened and bubbly. Stir in celery seed, Worcestershire sauce, tuna and salt. Heat through. Add cheese. Heat until melted.

Betty Wade

- 2 medium carrots (1 cup shredded)
- 1 medium onion (½ cup chopped)
- ¼ cup butter
- ¼ cup flour
- 2 cups milk
- 2 cups chicken broth
- 1 6½ ounce can tuna (drained)
- ½ teaspoon celery seed
- ½ teaspoon Worcestershire sauce
- ¼ teaspoon salt
- 1 cup shredded American cheese

Cure/Remedy for Pneumonia

Take 6 or 8 large onions, chop fine. Put in pan over the fire and pour in some vinegar, about a pint. While it is simmering, thicken with flour, until it makes a good thick poultice. Spread on cheese cloth and apply it as hot as can be borne on patients chest. A good test is to apply poultice to your own cheeks. As soon as it gets a little cool, put another one one. A good plan is to have one in the oven all the time between 2 pie plates. Two poultices will last for 2 or 3 hours and may be kept moist with vinegar.

Gertrude Guise

Cabbage and Kielbasa Soup

Serves Twenty to Twenty-four

Drop into Diener's Restaurant on Tuesdays to sample this hearty and robust soup.

- 1½ cups chopped celery
- 1½ cups chopped onions
- 1½ cups chopped carrots
- 3 tablespoons beef bouillon
- 2 teaspoons dried basil
- 1 teaspoon dried oregano
- ½ teaspoon pepper
- 8 cups water
- 4 cups stewed tomatoes
- 1 46 ounce can of V-8 Juice
- ½ head finely chopped cabbage
- 8 cups Kielbasa, sliced ¼ inch thick

In a large kettle, combine first 7 ingredients with water. Cook, covered, until vegetables are tender. Add tomatoes, juice, cabbage and Kielbasa. Simmer an additional 30 minutes.

Judy Hall

Vegetable Soup

Serves Fourteen to Sixteen

Four generations have found this soup to be a perfect way to feed vegetables to their families.

Add the tomatoes, onion, corn, celery, shin bones and cabbage to cold water in a large soup pot. Cook for one hour. Add the mixed vegetables and bouillon and simmer for 1½ hours. Add the potatoes and simmer for ½ hour. During the last 15 minutes add the noodles, salt, pepper, thyme and parsley.

Sarah Haddock Masland

Note
The soup simmers for a total of 3 hours.

12	cups cold water
1	can tomatoes
1	medium onion, sliced
1	can cream style corn
3	ribs celery, sliced
2	rounds of shin bone with meat
1	cup cabbage, shredded, (optional)
2	large bags of frozen mixed vegetables
2	beef bouillon cubes
7-8	potatoes, peeled and diced
2-3	handfuls thin noodles
1	teaspoon salt
¼	teaspoon pepper
1	teaspoon thyme
1	tablespoon parsley

At left, **West Main Street**
*Horse and carriage in front of what is now
Diener's Restaurant
Mechanicsburg
1900*

-Mechanicsburg Museum Association

Italian Sausage Soup

Serves Eight to Ten

Serve with a robust red wine and a good crusty bread.

- 1½ pounds sweet Italian sausage
- 1½ cups chopped onions
- 1 28 ounce can Italian-style tomatoes
- 3 cans (14 ounces each) beef broth
- 1½ cups water or dry red wine
- 1 teaspoon basil leaves
- ¼ teaspoon pepper
- 2 medium zucchini, sliced
- 1½ cups pasta (rotelle, ruffles, etc.)
- 1 medium green pepper, diced
- ¼ cup parsley
- Parmesan cheese

Remove casing from sausage. Cut in ½ inch lengths and brown in heavy 6 quart pan over medium heat. Discard all but 1 tablespoon of the drippings. Add onions, and cook 5 minutes. Add tomatoes, basil, water and pepper. Cover and simmer 30 minutes. Stir in rest of ingredients and simmer 30 minutes. Serve with Parmesan cheese.

Joan Jurgensen

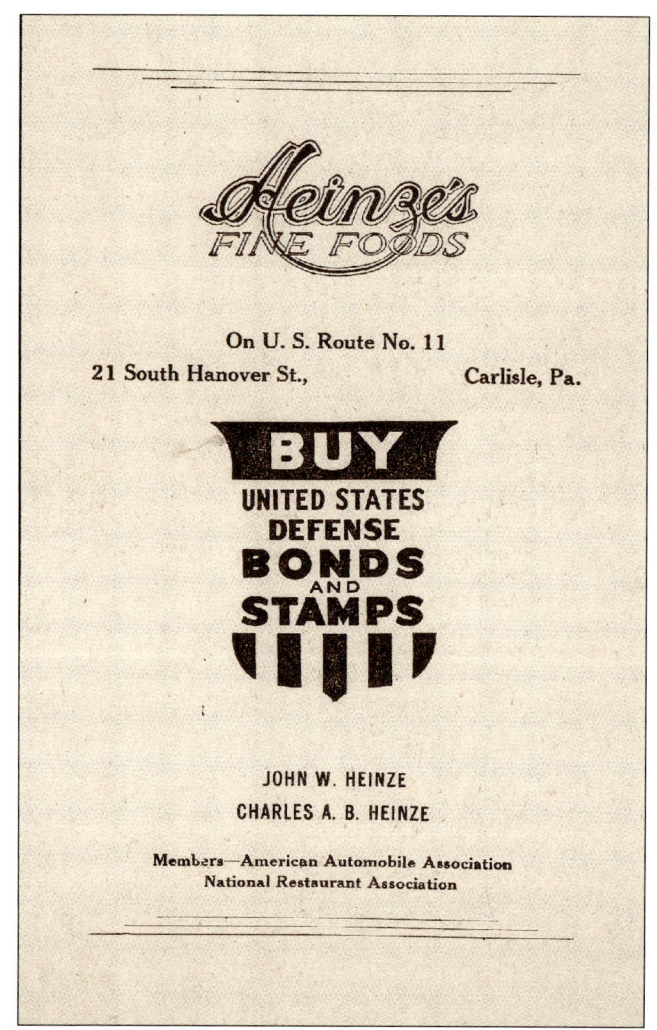

Hamburger Soup

Serves Four to Six

Sure to be a hit with your family.

Brown meat and drain off fat. Add the rest of the ingredients. Bring to a boil, then simmer covered for one hour or until vegetables are tender. Season with salt and pepper to taste. Remove bay leaf. Can be frozen.

Marjorie Mowery

1	pound hamburger
5	cups water
2	medium carrots, sliced
1/3	cup pearl barley
1	tablespoon beef bouillion
1	teaspoon basil
1	bay leaf
1	(16 oz.) can tomatoes, cut up
2	medium onions, chopped
2	stalks celery, sliced
1/4	cup catsup
2	teaspoons seasoned salt

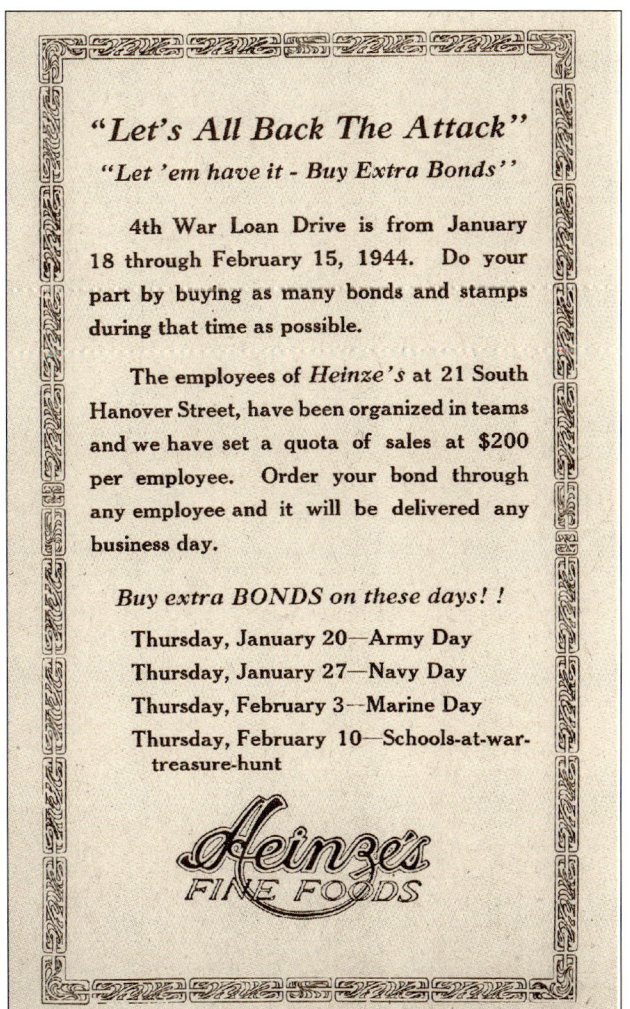

At left and far left, **Menu Cover**
21 South Hanover Street
Carlisle
1944

-CCHS, donated by Jean Ritter

Tortellini Soup

For a vegetarian soup, omit the sausage.

- 2 cloves garlic, crushed
- 1 tablespoon olive oil
- 1 quart chicken broth
- 8 ounces cheese tortellini
- 10 ounces chopped spinach, thawed
- 16 ounces Italian flavored tomatoes, undrained, coarsely chopped
- 8 ounces cooked Italian sausage, drained and thinly sliced
- freshly grated Parmesan or Romano cheese

In a large saucepan over medium heat, sauté garlic in oil for 2 to 3 minutes. Add broth and bring to a boil. Reduce heat to low and add all other ingredients. Simmer 15 to 20 minutes. Serve with freshly grated Parmesan or Romano cheese.

Judy Castrina
Donna Landis

Stambaugh's Dairy
*118 West North Street
Carlisle
1948*

-CCHS, Steinmetz Collection

Vegetarian Chili

Serves Six

F*or those meatless meals, this can't be beat.*

About 45 minutes before serving, prepare macaroni as label directs, omiting salt. Drain and set aside. Meanwhile, in 5-quart Dutch oven over medium-high heat, cook carrots and onions in oil, stirring occasionally, until vegetables begin to brown. Add zucchini and yellow squash and cook until all vegetables are tender-crisp. Stir in chili powder and salt. Cook one minute. Add tomatoes, corn, chopped green chilies, with their liquids, tomato paste, hot pepper sauce, and 2 cups water. Heat to boiling. Reduce heat to low and simmer, uncovered for 20 minutes. Stir in beans and macaroni. Heat through.

June Trinnaman

- 1 cup elbow macaroni
- 2 tablespoons salad oil
- 2 medium-size carrots, thinly sliced
- 1 large onion, chopped
- 1 medium-size zucchini, cut into 1/2 inch pieces
- 1 medium-size yellow straight neck squash, cut into 1/2 inch pieces
- 2 tablespoons chili powder
- 1/2 teaspoon salt
- 1 28-ounce can tomatoes, undrained
- 1 16-ounce can whole-kernel corn, undrained
- 1 4-ounce can chopped mild green chilies, undrained
- 1/3 cup tomato paste
- 1/4 teaspoon hot pepper sauce
- 2 15 1/4 to 19 ounce cans red kidney beans, rinsed and drained

White Chili

Serves Eight

This chili is enhanced when served with the suggested condiments.

1	pound large white beans, soaked over night in water, drained
6	cups chicken broth
2	cloves garlic, minced
2	medium onions, chopped, (divided)
1	tablespoon oil
2	4 ounce cans chopped (mild or medium) green chilies
2	teaspoons ground cumin
1½	teaspoons dried oregano
¼	teaspoon ground cloves
¼	teaspoon cayenne pepper
4	cups diced cooked chicken breasts
3	cups grated Monterey Jack cheese

Combine beans, chicken broth, garlic and half of the onions in a large soup pot and bring to a boil. Reduce heat and simmer until beans are very soft, 3 hours or more. Add more chicken broth, if necessary. In a skillet, sauté remaining onions in oil until tender. Add chilies and seasonings and mix thoroughly. Add to bean mixture. Add chicken and continue to simmer 1 hour. Serve topped with grated cheese.

Nancy Wilson

Note

For a Southwest buffet, serve with chopped tomatoes, chopped cilantro or parsley, chopped olives, guacamole, sour cream, crumbled tortilla chips and salsa.

At right, **Frycklunds**
South College Street at Walnut Bottom Road
Carlisle
c. 1930

-CCHS, Ravenda Frycklund Collection

Mushroom Vegetable Soup

Serves Six

Even better reheated the next day.

Sauté mushrooms, carrots, celery, tomato, onion and garlic in oil and margarine until vegetables are tender-crisp. Stir in beef broth, water, barley and seasonings. Simmer for 30 minutes.

Rita Schlansky

- 3 cups sliced mushrooms
- 1 cup shredded carrots
- 1 cup sliced celery
- 1 large tomato, chopped
- 1 medium onion, chopped
- 1 clove garlic, pressed
- 2 tablespoons butter or margarine
- 2 tablespoons vegetable or canola oil
- 2 13 ounce cans beef broth
- 2 cups water
- ½ cup pearl barley
- ½ teaspoon thyme, crumbled
- ½ teaspoon salt

Oatmeal Soup

Serves Four to Six

Try this morning, 'noon', or night.

- 2 tablespoons butter
- 1 large onion, minced
- 4-5 cloves garlic, minced
- 1 cup old fashioned oatmeal (not instant)
- 2 quarts chicken stock
- 1 14.5 ounce can stewed tomatoes
- 2 teaspoons parsley
- ¾ teaspoon salt
- ¾ teaspoon coarse pepper

In soup pot, brown onion and garlic in butter. Add oatmeal and chicken stock. Cook for 15 to 20 minutes. Add parsley, salt, pepper, and stewed tomatoes. Simmer 15 to 20 minutes.

Zell Todd

Pumpkin Pecan Soup

Serves Eight

For an elegant first course, serve in a small scooped out pumpkin or acorn squash.

- 2 cups canned pumpkin
- 1 large onion, diced
- 2 cups chicken broth
- ½ cup maple syrup
- ¼ cup pecans, roasted and chopped
- 1 teaspoon cinnamon
- 1 teaspoon nutmeg
- 2 tablespoons butter
- ½ cup heavy cream
- salt and white pepper

Sauté onions in butter. Add pumpkin, chicken broth, maple syrup, nuts and spices and simmer 30 minutes. Let cool, pour in food processor and puree. Add cream and stir till smooth. Add salt and white pepper to taste. Reheat gently for serving. Garnish with sour cream and chopped scallions or pecan halves.

Pat Strickler

Cream Of Potato Soup

Serves Six to Eight

For a change of pace, add two fresh leeks in place of the onion.

Combine first eight ingredients and cook on medium low heat for 30 minutes. Mash slightly. Add mashed eggs, margarine and hot milk. Blend well and serve with small crackers. Garnish with chopped parsley or chopped hard boiled egg for color.

Hilda Arnold

- 3 cups water
- 4 large potatoes, pared and sliced
- 1 large onion, cut fine
- 2 ribs celery, diced
- 1 teaspoon salt
- dash of pepper
- ¼ cup parsley flakes or ½ cup fresh
- 2 chicken bouillon cubes
- 2 hard boiled eggs, mashed
- 2 tablespoons margarine
- 4 cups hot milk

Potage Saint-Cloud

Serves Twelve

A creamy green pea soup as smooth and as rich as melted ice cream.

Melt butter. Sauté onion, garlic, potatoes, carrots, turmeric and curry until onion is wilted. Add broth and simmer until the largest chunk of carrot is tender. Add peas and keep simmering for 10 minutes. In a food processor, puree all solids and return to broth. Add cream and season with salt and pepper.

Oliver Hazan

- ½ stick butter
- 2 onions, chopped coarsely
- 2 cloves garlic
- 3 or 4 potatoes, peeled and quartered
- 2 carrots, sliced
- 1 teaspoon turmeric
- 1 tablespoon curry powder
- 6 cups chicken broth
- 1 pound frozen peas
- ¾ cup heavy cream

Iced Cucumber Soup

Serves Four to Six

Refreshing on a hot day.

- 1 medium cucumber
- 1 cup chicken broth
- 1 ½ inch slice of a medium onion
- ¾ teaspoon salt
- ¼-½ teaspoon dry mint leaves
- ⅛ teaspoon garlic powder
- ½ teaspoon lemon juice
- 1 cup sour cream
- 8 ounces plain yogurt

Peel cucumber and remove seeds; cut into thick slices. Put in blender container with broth, onion, seasonings and lemon juice. Blend until cucumber is grated, but not liquified. Combine sour cream and yogurt in bowl. Gradually stir in cucumber mixture. Blend well and refrigerate for one hour to enhance flavor. Serve in chilled cups or bowls. Garnish with chopped onion and/or a thin cucumber slice. Preparation time: 15 minutes.

Jan Hays

STRAWBERRY VELVET SOUP

Serves Six to Eight

Summer delight for your bridge group.

Combine strawberries, sugar and water in a saucepan. Bring to a boil and simmer 5 minutes. Stir in arrowroot water mixture, wine and juice. Bring mixture to a boil; cook stirring constantly, until slightly thickened. Cool 15 minutes. Pour into blender or food processor and puree. Stir in sour cream and chill. Serve garnished with sliced strawberries.

Ruth Bietsch

3	cups fresh strawberries, sliced
1	cup sugar
½	cup water
2	teaspoons arrowroot mixed with 1 tablespoon water
¾	cup rosé wine
1	cup fresh orange juice
1¼	cups sour cream
	fresh strawberries for garnish

SAVORY TOMATO SOUP

Makes Six Quarts

Keep this soup on hand in your freezer as a nice reminder of your summer tomato crop.

Cut vegetables into coarse pieces. Add other ingredients. Simmer 1½ to 2 hours. Strain through food mill. Put in blender. Freeze. If desired, add heavy cream and more butter before re-heating.

Virginia A. LaFond

At left, **Cutting Ice at Laurel Lake**
c. 1910
-CCHS

7	quarts tomatoes
4	onions
7	stalks celery
2	carrots
2	bunches parsley
1	clove garlic
1	tablespoon salt
2	bay leaves
½	cup brown sugar
1	teaspoon poultry seasoning
1	stick butter
1	cup flour
6	whole cloves
	few dashes red pepper

Cumberland Chicken Salad

Serves Four

One of the favorites at Allenberry.

- 2 cups cooked chicken meat, cut in half-inch cubes
- 2 tablespoons celery, chopped fine
- 4 hardcooked eggs, chopped
- 2 tablespoons red peppers, diced
- 1¼ teaspoons salt
- 1 teaspoon white pepper
- 2 teaspoons celery seed
- 2 tablespoons diced onion
- 1⅓ cups mayonnaise
- 3 tablespoons sweet pickle juice

Mix all ingredients carefully and gently using a wooden spoon. Chill and serve on crisp lettuce.

Jane Heinze

Overleaf, **Charlie Boova,** **Fruit and Vegetable Stand**
King Street
Shippensburg
c. 1913

-Shippensburg Historical Society Collection

Harvest Time in a County Orchard
c. 1920
A. A. Line photographer

-CCHS

72 PAST RECEIPTS PRESENT RECIPES

Dilled Apple-Chicken Salad

Serves Four

Grapes and dill add fresh Spring tastes.

Place chicken breast halves on plate. Cover with wax paper. Microwave on high 5 minutes or until done, rotating half way. Cut into bite sized chunks. Combine mayonnaise, dill, lemon juice and salt and pepper. Mix well. In a large bowl, combine chicken, apples, celery, grapes. Add dressing. Just before serving add nuts. Arrange lettuce leaves on plates and top with salad.

Judy Castrina

- 2 boneless, skinless chicken breast halves
- 2 Granny Smith apples, cored and chopped
- 2 celery stalks, diced
- 1 cup seedless green or red grapes, halved
- ½ cup low-fat mayonnaise
- 2 tablespoons fresh chopped dill
- 1½ tablespoons lemon juice
- ½ teaspoon salt
- ⅛ teaspoon black pepper
- ½ cup nuts, shelled pistachios, pecans, macadamia—your choice
- Boston lettuce leaves

FRUITED CHICKEN AND RICE SALAD

Serves Eight

Pretty to look at, delicious to eat.

- 1 package Near East rice pilaf
- ½ cup mayonnaise
- ¼ cup sour cream
- ½ cup orange marmalade
- 3 tablespoons lemon juice
- 1½ teaspoons curry powder
- 3 cups cubed cooked chicken
- 1 large Red Delicious apple, cubed (skin on)
- ½ cup raisins or dried cranberries
- ¾ cup toasted slivered almonds

Prepare pilaf, chill. Combine mayonnaise, sour cream, marmalade, lemon juice and curry. Add chicken, apples and raisins to pilaf. Add dressing and mix well. Chill. Serve on greens and garnish with almonds.

Anne Pass

At right and far right, **Menu American Restaurant** 123 West High Street Carlisle

-CCHS

Hot Chicken Salad

Serves Six

An easy make ahead dish.

Mix all ingredients except for the topping of cheese, chips and almonds. Place in a 9x13 inch pan and add the topping. Cover and let stand overnight in the refrigerator. Preheat oven to 400°. Bake for 20 to 25 minutes.

Margaret E. MacGregor

4	cups cooked chicken, cooled and cut in chunks
1	cup chopped celery
4	hard boiled eggs, chopped
2	teaspoons lemon juice
¾	cup mayonnaise
1	teaspoon salt
1	small minced onion
1	can cream of chicken soup, undiluted
1	cup grated sharp Cheddar cheese
1½	cups crushed potato chips
⅔	cup chopped almonds, toasted

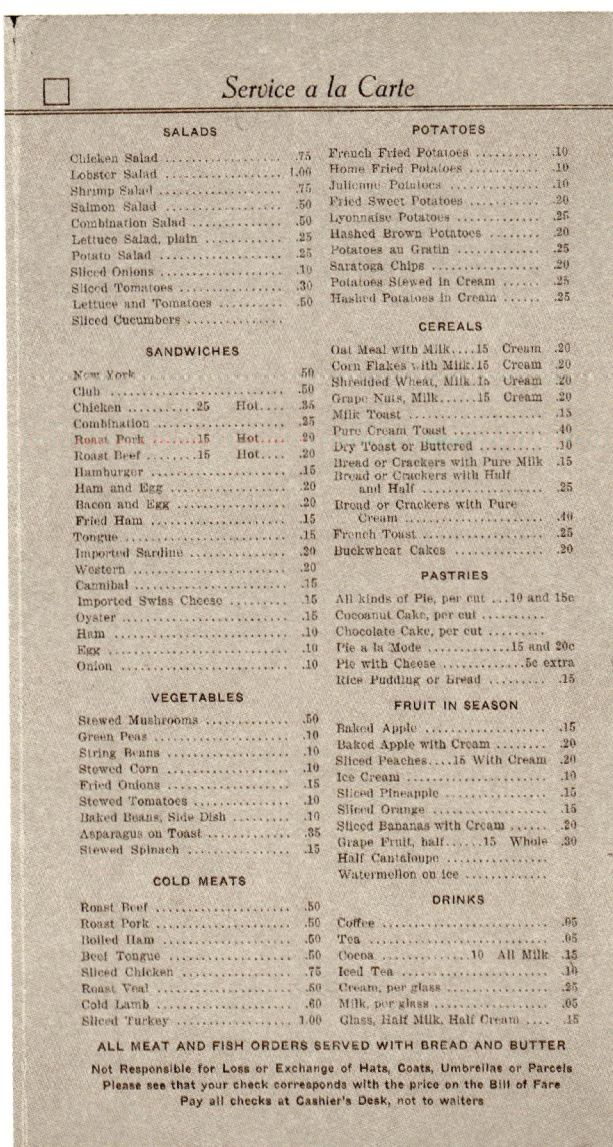

Salads 75

Regal Chicken Salad

Serves Eight to Ten

Recipe courtesy of the Cumberland County Office of the Blind.

- 4 cups diced, cooked chicken
- 1 20½ ounce can of pineapple tidbits, drained (reserve juice)
- 2 cups seedless green grapes
- 1 cup chopped celery
- 1 cup mayonnaise
- 2 tablespoons lemon juice
- 2 tablespoons pineapple juice
- ¼ teaspoon crushed tarragon
- ⅔ cup dry salted peanuts (optional)

Combine the chicken, pineapple, grapes, celery, and peanuts. Stir in the tarragon. Salt to taste. In another bowl, combine the mayonnaise, lemon juice and reserved pineapple juice. Fold this mixture into the chicken-fruit mixture. Chill.

Ruth Diffenderfer

New Orleans Crab Salad

Serves Eight or More

A great way to stretch expensive crab meat with rich results.

Mix all together and refrigerate overnight. Serve surrounded by mixed salad greens.

Gwen Wood

- 1 pound crab meat
- 2 cups cooked small pasta shells
- 1 cup chopped celery
- 1/2 cup chopped red or green pepper
- 1 cup mayonnaise
- 1/4 cup flat beer
- 1/4 teaspoon curry powder
- 1 teaspoon salt
- 1 teaspoon lemon juice
- 1/4 teaspoon dry mustard
- 1 teaspoon minced onion

Celebration Shrimp Salad

Serves Twelve

Shrimply delicious.

One to eight hours before serving, mix all of the ingredients in a large bowl. Refrigerate immediately. Serve on broken pieces of Romaine or iceberg lettuce.

Betty Cornman Weary

- 4 cups cooked bite-sized shrimp
- 3 cups diced celery
- 2 cups sliced stuffed olives
- 1/2 cup fat free French dressing
- 1/2 cup low fat mayonnaise
- 1/2 cup minced, raw onion
  salt, pepper, seafood seasoning, to taste

At left, Cresslers Fruit Market
209 West King Street
Shippensburg
c. 1935

-Shippensburg Historical Society Collection

SALADS

Black Bean Salad

Serves Six

Great for a Bar-B-Que crowd.

For the Salad

- 2   15 ounce cans black beans
- 1   11 ounce can white shoepeg corn, drained
- 1-2 bunches green onions, diced
- ½   yellow pepper, diced
- ½   red pepper, diced
- 1-3 jalapeño peppers, diced
- 1   tablespoon cilantro, optional

For the Dressing

- 2   tablespoons vinegar
- 1   teaspoon salt
- 2   teaspoons Dijon mustard
- ½   teaspoon pepper
- 6   tablespoons olive oil
      diced tomatoes

Toss salad ingredients together. For dressing, whisk salt and pepper in vinegar, add mustard, slowly add oil. Add diced tomatoes at time of serving.

Patti Owen

DINING HALL-DOUBLING

Sweet Pickle Bean Salad

Serves Six

Simple and great for summer—no cooking.

Mix lightly, cover bowl, chill several hours and drain.

Wayne Rutz

2 cups pre-cooked red kidney beans, drained
2 cups pre-cooked cut green beans, drained
1 cup sugar
1 cup vinegar
1 cup sweet pickle relish
1 large red onion, sliced
⅓ cup salad or olive oil

Doubling Gap Hotel
Newville
c. 1910
Maynard Hoover, Photographer

-CCHS

Broccoli, Snow Pea And Baby Corn Salad

Serves Four to Six

U*nusual and colorful.*

For the Salad:

- 2 cups chopped broccoli florets
- 1 cup fresh snow peas, cut in half
- ½ cup sliced red onion
- ½ medium sweet red pepper, sliced
- ¾ cup drained mandarin orange sections
- ½ cup sliced water chestnuts
- 8 drained baby corn cobs, cut in half if large
- 1-2 tablespoons raisins
- 1 tablespoon chopped walnuts
- 3 cups torn greens (Romaine, Red Leaf, etc.)

For the Dressing:

- 3 tablespoons olive oil
- 3 tablespoons frozen orange juice concentrate, thawed
- 1½ teaspoons red wine vinegar
- ½ teaspoon crushed garlic
- 4 teaspoons lemon juice
- 1 teaspoon granulated sugar

Combine all dressing ingredients. Can be prepared up to one day ahead. Combine all salad ingredients, except greens. Arrange greens in salad bowl or on a large platter. Pour dressing over vegetable mixture and toss well. Arrange on top of greens.

Eve Wilkie

Broccoli Salad

Serves Eight to Ten

Flavor is enhanced by preparing one day ahead.

Thoroughly mix the salad ingredients. Then mix the dressing ingredients and pour the dressing over the salad. May mix a day in advance and marinate or mix just before serving.

Jean L. Saam
Jack W. Wise

For the Salad

1	large bunch broccoli
½	cup chopped red onion
5-6	slices bacon - cooked crisp and crumbled
½	cup golden raisins
¾	cup sunflower seed kernels

For the Dressing

¾	cup mayonnaise
1½	tablespoons vinegar
¼	cup sugar

**Vegetable Garden,
Mr. W. H. Shoemaker**
*Beetem Carpet Factory
Carlisle
June, 1920
A.A. Line, photographer*

-CCHS

SALADS 81

Fruited Couscous Salad

Serves Four to Six

Very good served over greens.

- 1 cup couscous
- 1 cup fresh orange juice
- ½ cup water
- ¼ olive oil
- 1 tablespoon wine vinegar
- 8 dried apricots, thinly sliced
- 1 tablespoon dried currants
- 1 tablespoon golden raisins
- 2 teaspoons grated fresh ginger
- ¼ teaspoon salt
- ½ cup finely chopped red onion
- 2 tablespoons pine nuts, toasted

Put couscous into a small mixing bowl. Combine orange juice, water, oil and vinegar in a small saucepan. Bring just to a boil and add fruit, ginger and salt. Pour immediately over couscous. Cover and let sit for 20 minutes. Bring a small pan of water to a boil and drop in chopped red onion for 15 seconds. Drain well and toss with a few splashes of vinegar to draw out the pink color. Fluff couscous with a fork and toss with pine nuts and onion.

Anne Pass

Greek Salad

Serves Six to Eight

Food in Cumberland County has been strongly influenced by the Greek community.

For the Salad

greens– any combination of
lettuce, spinach, romaine, shredded carrots, shredded red cabbage, sliced radishes, tomatoes or cherry tomatoes
Greek olives
Feta cheese

For the Dressing

- ½ cup oil
- ⅓ cup wine vinegar
- 1½ teaspoon salt
- 1½ teaspoon oregano

Combine dressing ingredients into jar and shake well. Toss over greens at last minute. Top with chunks of Feta.

Gretchen Hoffman

Johnson Food Market
Paul Johnson and Robert Frey
161 South Hanover Street
Carlisle
1953

-CCHS, Steinmetz Collection

Perfection Salad

Serves Eight

A classic American recipe from the turn of the century.

- 2 tablespoons Knox gelatin
- 1 cup cold water
- ½ cup white vinegar
- 2 tablespoons lemon juice
- 2 cups boiling water
- ½ cup sugar
- 1 teaspoon salt
- 1 cup shredded cabbage
- 2 cups diced celery
- ¼ cup chopped red and green peppers
- 1 large onion, chopped fine

Soak gelatin in cold water; add vinegar, lemon juice, boiling water, sugar and salt. When mixture begins to thicken, add vegetables and turn into a mold.

Ann Morris Blumenthal
Jean Morris Portmann

Johnson Food Market
Paul Johnson and Robert Frey
161 South Hanover Street
Carlisle
1953

-CCHS, Steinmetz Collection

Lowensahn (Dandelion) Salad

Serves Four

This salad was served in the spring when Grandmother would gather tender, young dandelions from the garden.

For the Salad

- 4 cups chopped dandelion greens
- 3 hard-cooked eggs, chopped
- 3 slices of fried bacon, chopped

For the Dressing

- bacon drippings
- 1½ tablespoons flour
- 2 tablespoons sugar
- 1 teaspoon salt
- ¼ cup vinegar
- 1 egg
- 2 cups milk or water

Gently toss salad ingredients. To prepare dressing, mix all ingredients, cook until thickened, let cool slightly and pour over the salad.

Wayne Rutz

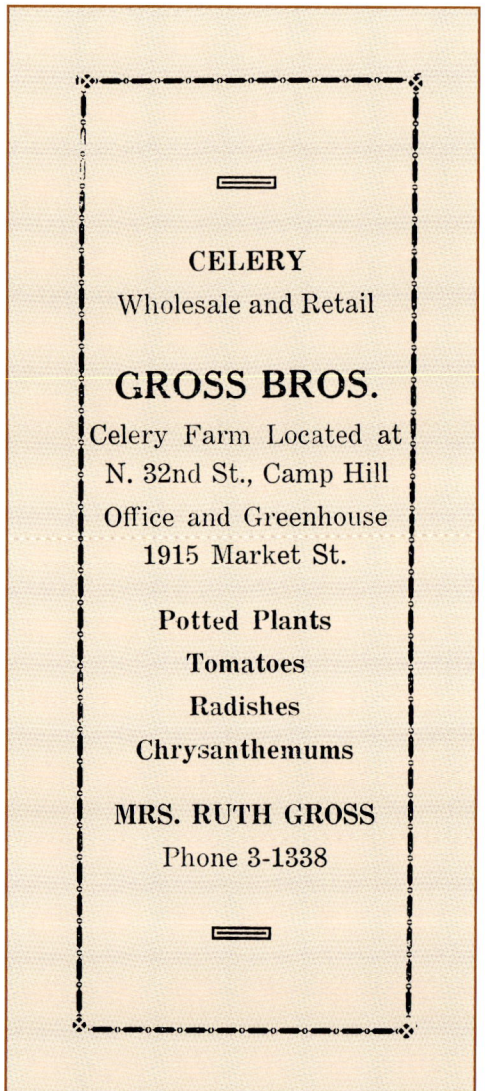

Cumberland County Directory Ad
Camp Hill
1931
-CCHS

ITALIAN VEGETABLE & PASTA TOSS

Serves Ten to Twelve

An *attractive alternative is tri-colored rotini.*

Toss all together except avocado, tomato and mushrooms. Chill thoroughly. Just before serving, top with tomato, avocado and mushroom slices.

Isabelle Hazlett

Note
This salad will be more attractive if the chopped and sliced ingredients are uniform in size.

1½	cups rotini, cooked and drained
2	cups broccoli florets
1	cup cauliflower florets
1	cup sliced mushrooms
1	medium avocado, sliced
1	medium tomato, seeded and sliced
1	16 ounce jar artichoke hearts, rinsed, drained and chopped
1	cup sliced ripe olives
½	cup green onion, small slice
⅔	cup Italian salad dressing
¼	pound pepperoni, chopped
¼	pound salami, chopped
¼	pound provolone cheese, chopped

Dandelion Juice

Corns may be removed by applying the milky juice of common dandelion.

Gertrude Guise

SALADS

Wild Rice Salad

Serves Ten to Twelve

Wonderful served with grilled meats.

For the Salad

- 1/2 pound fresh mushrooms sliced
- juice of 1 lemon
- 1/2 pound wild rice cooked and drained
- 4 green onions, sliced thin
- 1 red bell pepper, chopped
- salt and pepper
- 2 cups frozen tiny peas, thawed

For the Dressing

- 6 garlic cloves minced
- 2 teaspoons Dijon mustard
- 1 teaspoon salt
- 1/2 teaspoon pepper
- 1/4 cup Champagne vinegar
- 1/2 cup vegetable oil
- 1 teaspoon fresh tarragon or 1/4 teaspoon dried tarragon
- 1/4 teaspoon sugar

Combine mushroom and lemon juice in a large bowl. Add rice, onion and red pepper. Combine dressing ingredients and mix well. Add to rice mixture and toss lightly, seasoning with salt and pepper. Toss in peas one hour before serving and serve at room temperature.

Rosalie George

Note

Wine vinegar may be substituted for the Champagne vinegar and a combination of wild and white rice may be used.

Orzo Salad

Serves Six

Prepare this for your next Tailgate.

Cook orzo according to package directions. Rinse with cold water, cool and set aside. Mix dressing of olive oil, lemon juice, salt and pepper to taste. Add remaining ingredients to orzo. Add dressing and toss well. This is best if made ahead of time (at least a few hours or overnight).

June Slep

1	cup orzo
⅔	cup olive oil, scant
⅓	cup fresh lemon juice
¼	cup green onions, minced
2	tablespoons chopped parsley
6	ounces Feta cheese, crumbled
3-4	tablespoons pine nuts, toasted
	salt and pepper

W. H. Miller and His Goats
April, 1918
A. A. Line photographer
-CCHS

SALADS

Pat's Potato Salad

Serves Ten to Twelve

Tomato roses and parsley garnish make a nice addition to this potato salad.

- 2½ pounds potatoes
- 3 eggs
- 2 tablespoons flour
- 9 tablespoons vinegar
- 4 tablespoons water
- ¾ cup sugar
- 2 tablespoons butter
- 1 teaspoon salt
- ½ cup chopped celery
- ½ cup chopped onion
- 2 tablespoons parsley flakes
- 2 cups mayonnaise

Cook and dice potatoes. Make a dressing by mixing eggs, sugar, flour, salt, vinegar, water and butter together. Cook until thick. Thin with mayonnaise. Add onion, celery and parsley. Pour over potatoes. Mix gently and chill.

Patricia Lehman

German Potato Salad

Serves Five to Seven

**A** family recipe served at Thanksgiving and Christmas along with Mashed Potatoes and Stuffing.

For the Salad
- 1 pound potatoes
- ½ cup chopped onion, ¼ inch dice
- ½ cup chopped celery, ¼ inch dice
- capers (preferably small size)

For the Dressing
- 1 cup vinegar
- ½ cup olive oil
- ⅛ cup sugar
- salt and pepper
- 2 teaspoons celery seed

Peel and boil potatoes (not too tender). Slice ¼ inch thick. Combine potatoes, celery and onions in a flat glass roasting pan. Mix dressing ingredients in a separate bowl and pour over the potato mixture, stirring gently, trying not to break up the potato slices. Refrigerate overnight. Just before serving, add capers.

Rosa Willimeck

Note
This potato salad is good for picnics as it contains no mayonnaise.

Spinach Salad

Serves Four

Serve with your favorite entree.

Mix salad ingredients together. Mix dressing. Just before serving, pour over salad and toss.

Susan McCrea

For the Salad

- 6 handfuls or cups fresh spinach leaves, washed and dried
- ¾ lb. or 1 cup sliced mushrooms
- 3 slices cooked crumbled bacon
- ½ cup sliced red onion
- ¼ cup Bleu cheese

For the Dressing

- 1 tablespoon lemon juice
- ¾ teaspoon Dijon mustard
- 3 tablespoons olive oil
- salt and pepper

Spinach Waldorf Salad

Serves Six

Cooked and cubed chicken breasts makes this a more substantial salad.

Combine all salad ingredients in a serving bowl. Blend dressing ingredients throroughly. Dress salad gently.

Eve Wilkie

Note
Commercially prepared Poppyseed dressing may be substituted for the Honey Mustard dressing.

For the Salad

- 8 ounces fresh spinach
- 1 red apple, cored and cubed
- 2 stalks celery, diced
- ½ cup seedless red grapes, halved
- 3 tablespoons chopped walnuts
- 3 tablespoons raisins

Honey Mustard Dressing

- ¼ cup red wine vinegar
- ½ cup olive oil
- 3 tablespoons honey
- 2 tablespoons Dijon mustard

Crunchy Spinach Cabbage Salad

Serves Two

Not your ordinary Spinach Salad.

For the Salad
- 2 cups fresh spinach, torn
- 1/2 cup finely shredded red cabbage
- 2 tablespoons raisins
- 2 tablespoons sliced toasted almonds
- 2 cups water
- 1/4 cup white vinegar

For the Dressing
- 2 tablespoons sugar
- 1/4 teaspoon salt
- 1/4 teaspoon dry mustard
- 1/4 teaspoon celery seed
- 2 teaspoons chopped onion
- 2 tablespoons cider vinegar
- 1/4 cup vegetable oil

Bring white vinegar and water to a boil. Add red cabbage and boil 2 to 3 minutes. Drain and chill. Toss spinach and red cabbage at serving time. Shake dressing and toss lightly. Top with almonds and raisins.

Joyce Nelson

Note:
This recipe can be increased easily.

Splendid Strawberry Spinach Salad
Serves Eight

Equally good when you substitute raspberries for the vinegar, jam and fruit.

TO MAKE THE DRESSING
Combine vinegar and jam in a blender or small bowl. Add oil in a thin stream, blending well. Add salt.

TO MAKE THE SALAD
Toss spinach, ½ of nuts, ½ of strawberries and ½ of kiwis with dressing. Top with remaining nuts, strawberries and kiwis. Serve immediately.

Debbie Masland

For the Dressing
- 2 tablespoons strawberry vinegar
- 2 tablespoons strawberry jam
- ⅓ cup vegetable oil
- ¼ teaspoon salt

For the Salad
- 8 cups spinach, washed, stemmed and torn into bite size pieces
- ¾ cup coarsely chopped Macadamia nuts
- 1 cup fresh strawberries, halved
- 3 kiwis, peeled and sliced

Fogelsanger Grocery Store
L to R: David, William and Lamar Fogelsanger
Shippensburg
c. 1908

-Shippensburg Historical Society Collection

ENDIVE, WATERCRESS & POMEGRANATE SALAD

Serves Six

Improvise: substitute spinach for watercress and dried cranberries for pomegranate seeds.

- 1 pomegranate, halved and seeds removed
- 1 large scallion, thinly sliced into rounds
- 1 bunch watercress, washed, dried and tough stems removed
- 4 medium Belgian endives, cut into 1 inch pieces
- 1 tablespoon red wine vinegar
- 3 tablespoons light olive oil
- salt and pepper to taste

Reserve ¼ cup pomegranate seeds for salad; eat the remaining seeds. Combine watercress and endive. Refrigerate. Whisk vinegar, oil, salt and pepper in a small bowl. At serving time, arrange greens, sprinkle scallion rings and pomegranate seeds on top. Dress with vinaigrette.

Sandy Gority

Note

This makes a lovely holiday salad when pomegranates are in season.

A Refreshing Way to Prepare Lettuce

Take a nicely blanched head of lettuce, cut into 4 quarters, leaving enough of the stem to cause the leaves of each quarter to hold together. Serve ½ a lemon with each quarter.

Sprinkle salt on the lettuce then squeeze over the lemon juice.

This is particularly refreshing on a warm morning for breakfast or for luncheon during the heated season.

In making salads of lettuce with either french or mayonnaise dressing, the addition of a handful of nasturtium flowers cannot be over-estimated. Not only is the appearance of the dish enhanced but the pungent flavor is refreshing and delightful.

When french dressing is used the addition to a bowl of lettuce of the smaller, finer nasturtium leaves as well as flowers is excellent.

Peachy Parker's Cookbook

Low Cal Vegetable Slaw

Serves Eight

Still tangy and refreshing after 100 years.

Combine all ingredients except cabbage in a medium sized pan. Bring to boil for several minutes. Allow to cool. Cut up small chunks of solid, green cabbage, placing them in the blender, covering with cold water. Process briefly, until fine or coarse, whichever you prefer. When finished, pour contents into a colander resting in a large bowl. Repeat until whole head of cabbage has been used. Allow to stand, tilting bowl several times to drain off excess water. Chop other vegetables desired in salad, such as green peppers, red peppers, celery, and carrots. Blend with cabbage and cooled liquid. Allow slaw to stand several hours before serving.

Katie Weaver

- 1 head of green cabbage
- 1 cup white vinegar
- 1 cup granulated sugar
- ¼ cup water
- 1 teaspoon celery seed
- 1 teaspoon mustard seed
- 1 teaspoon salt

No-Mayo Cole Slaw

Serves Four to Six

Pack-a-punch cole slaw.

Combine first six ingredients. Add vinegar, sour cream and caraway seed, and mix well. When ready to serve, mix dressing with cabbage.

Suzanne Phillippe

- 1 teaspoon seasoned salt
- 1 tablespoon sugar
- 1 tablespoon chopped basil
- ¾ teaspoon hot prepared mustard
- 4 tablespoons chopped chives or green onion tops
- 2 tablespoons white wine vinegar
- ½ cup sour cream
- ¾ teaspoon caraway seed, crushed
- 4 cups chopped or shredded cabbage

Simply Super Tomatoes

Serves Six

Wonderful with vine ripened tomatoes.

- 6 medium tomatoes, cut in ½" slices
- ⅔ cup oil
- ¼ cup wine vinegar
- ¼ cup finely chopped parsley
- ¼ cup finely chopped green onions
- 1 garlic clove minced
- 1 teaspoon salt
- 1 teaspoon dill weed
- 1 teaspoon basil leaves
- ½ teaspoon pepper

Arrange tomato slices in serving dish. In small bowl or jar with tight fitting lid, combine remaining ingredients; mix well. Pour some dressing over tomatoes. Cover; refrigerate 1-2 hours. Occasionally spoon dressing over tomatoes.

Marilyn Aust

Summer Cucumbers and Onions

Serves Six

Serve this with a spicy dish or a steak from the grill.

- 3 medium cucumbers peeled and thinly sliced
- 1 small Bermuda onion, thinly sliced
- 1 tablespoon sugar
- 1 teaspoon salt
- 4 teaspoons cider vinegar
- 1 cup sour cream
- ¼ teaspoon prepared mustard

Blend last 5 ingredients together. Add cucumbers and onion. Refrigerate at least 2 hours before serving.

Jane Heinze

At right, **Drinking Fountain on East Main Street at Franklin Hall**
Mechanicsburg
Gift of Women's Club in 1907

-CCHS

Zucchini Salad with Hot Bacon Dressing

Serves Six

 *A great use for all the summer squash.*

TO MAKE THE DRESSING:

Cook bacon in small skillet until crisp. Drain on paper towels, reserving 1 tablespoon drippings in skillet. Stir in sugar and cornstarch; add remaining dressing ingredients. Cook until mixture boils and thickens, stirring constantly. Set aside; cool slightly. Crumble cooked bacon.

TO MAKE THE SALAD:

In a large bowl, combine zucchini, onion and mushrooms; toss. Pour hot dressing over salad mixture; toss to coat. Arrange on salad greens, on individual plates, if desired. Garnish with tomatoes and bacon.

Eve Wilkie

For the Dressing

- 2 slices bacon
- 2 tablespoons sugar
- 2 teaspoons cornstarch
- ⅓ cup cider vinegar
- ⅓ cup water
- 1 teaspoon Worcestershire sauce
- ¼ teaspoon pepper

For the Salad

- 4 cups (4 medium) shredded zucchini
- ¼ cup finely chopped red onion
- 6 cherry tomatoes, halved
- 8 fresh mushrooms, sliced

Fountain, Mechanicsburg, Pa.

SALADS

Stuffed Cymlins with a Flavored Vinaigrette

Serves Four

This warm zucchini salad was a hit at the Candlelight Tavern Dinner at the Two Mile House.

- 4 whole baby zucchini
- 1 small sweet onion, sliced into at least 4 thin slices
- 2 tomatoes, sliced into at least 4 slices per tomato
- 4 slices provolone cheese
- 12 tablespoons olive oil
- 1 tablespoon balsamic vinegar
- 3 tablespoons red wine vinegar
- 2 tablespoons soy sauce
- juice of half of a lemon
- 1 teaspoon basil
- 1 teaspoon oregano
- 1 teaspoon salt
- 1 teaspoon fresh ground pepper
- 1 teaspoon garlic salt

Slice the zucchini lengthwise, three times, beginning at the round end, to about 1 inch before the stem end. Do not trim the ends. The zucchini will look like a fan. Place one onion slice in the middle slit, and one slice of tomato in each of the two outside slits. Preheat the oven to 350°. Make the vinaigrette dressing with the remaining ingredients. It is best to whisk the dressing. Place the zucchini stuffed with the tomato and onion in a roasting pan. Pour ⅓ of the dressing over the zucchini. Top with one slice of provolone cheese. Pour the remaining dressing over the cheese topped zucchini. Bake 5 to 8 minutes, depending on your preference. They should be al dente. Once they are done, serve on a plate and pour the warm vinaigrette dressing from the roasting pan on top.

Joe Luciano

WILTED GREENS WITH SWEET AND SOUR SAUCE
Serves Ten

You *may omit the egg if you like, but never the bacon.*

Fry bacon over high heat in saucepan or pot that is large enough to accommodate greens for tossing. Remove bacon bits when crisp. Drain on paper toweling. Add chopped onion to hot bacon drippings and reduce heat to medium. Cook onion 5 minutes, or until soft and golden. Add sugar and vinegar and cook at high heat until sugar is melted. Add greens and toss until wilted. Remove from heat to serving dish and garnish with bacon and egg. Serve immediately.

Tita Eberly

- 4 slices bacon, cut into 1 inch squares
- ⅓ onion, chopped
- ½ cup sugar
- ⅓ cup vinegar
- 3 quarts greens (spinach, chard, dandelion) washed and torn loosely into bite-size pieces
- 1 hard-boiled egg, grated or chopped

OLD FASHIONED WILTED LETTUCE
Serves Four

Just *like Grandmother used to make.*

Fry bacon until brown. Remove from pan and crumble. Beat egg with sugar, water and vinegar and add to drippings in pan. Let mixture come to a boil. Pour dressing over bacon and bite sized pieces of lettuce. Toss. Add salt as desired.

Margaret E. MacGregor

- 1 head leaf lettuce, torn into small pieces
- 2 strips bacon
- 1 egg
- 1 tablespoon sugar
- ¼ cup water
- ¼ cup vinegar
- salt to taste

At left, **Grocery Store, Wilber C. Landis**
Louther and West Streets
Carlisle
c. 1920

-CCHS

Perfection Salad

Serves Eight

A classic American recipe from the turn of the century.

- 2 tablespoons Knox gelatin
- 1 cup cold water
- ½ cup white vinegar
- 2 tablespoons lemon juice
- 2 cups boiling water
- ½ cup sugar
- 1 teaspoon salt
- 1 cup shredded cabbage
- 2 cups diced celery
- ¼ cup chopped red and green peppers
- 1 large onion, chopped fine

Soak gelatin in cold water; add vinegar, lemon juice, boiling water, sugar and salt. When mixture begins to thicken, add vegetables and turn into a mold.

Ann Morris Blumenthal
Jean Morris Portmann

Fruited Couscous Salad

Serves Four to Six

Very good served over greens.

- 1 cup couscous
- 1 cup fresh orange juice
- ½ cup water
- ¼ olive oil
- 1 tablespoon wine vinegar
- 8 dried apricots, thinly sliced
- 1 tablespoon dried currants
- 1 tablespoon golden raisins
- 2 teaspoons grated fresh ginger
- ¼ teaspoon salt
- ½ cup finely chopped red onion
- 2 tablespoons pine nuts, toasted

Put couscous into a small mixing bowl. Combine orange juice, water, oil and vinegar in a small saucepan. Bring just to a boil and add fruit, ginger and salt. Pour immediately over couscous. Cover and let sit for 20 minutes. Bring a small pan of water to a boil and drop in chopped red onion for 15 seconds. Drain well and toss with a few splashes of vinegar to draw out the pink color. Fluff couscous with a fork and toss with pine nuts and onion.

Anne Pass

Greek Salad

Serves Six to Eight

Food in Cumberland County has been strongly influenced by the Greek community.

For the Salad

greens– any combination of lettuce, spinach, romaine, shredded carrots, shredded red cabbage, sliced radishes, tomatoes or cherry tomatoes
Greek olives
Feta cheese

For the Dressing

- ½ cup oil
- ⅓ cup wine vinegar
- 1½ teaspoon salt
- 1½ teaspoon oregano

Combine dressing ingredients into jar and shake well. Toss over greens at last minute. Top with chunks of Feta.

Gretchen Hoffman

Broccoli Salad

Serves Eight to Ten

Flavor is enhanced by preparing one day ahead.

Thoroughly mix the salad ingredients. Then mix the dressing ingredients and pour the dressing over the salad. May mix a day in advance and marinate or mix just before serving.

Jean L. Saam
Jack W. Wise

For the Salad
- 1 large bunch broccoli
- ½ cup chopped red onion
- 5-6 slices bacon - cooked crisp and crumbled
- ½ cup golden raisins
- ¾ cup sunflower seed kernels

For the Dressing
- ¾ cup mayonnaise
- 1½ tablespoons vinegar
- ¼ cup sugar

Vegetable Garden, Mr. W. H. Shoemaker
*Beetem Carpet Factory
Carlisle
June, 1920
A.A. Line, photographer*

-CCHS

HOLIDAY SALAD

Serves Twelve or More

Good for holiday gatherings with the family.

Dissolve jello in 1¾ cup hot water. Mix remaining ingredients together with jello. Pour into a 9x13 inch pan. Chill until set. Serve in squares.

Margaret Steck Miller

- 1 large box orange jello
- 1 large can jellied cranberry sauce
- 1 large can crushed pineapple, drained
- 1 cup chopped nuts
- 1 teaspoon grated orange rind

ORANGE CREAM FRUIT SALAD

Serves Ten to Twelve

Tastes like a banana creamsicle.

Combine fruits, set aside. Combine pudding mix, milk and orange juice. Beat with electric mixer on low speed for 1 to 2 minutes until blended. Beat in sour cream. Fold into fruit mixture. Cover and chill.

Arlene Wentzel

Note

Best used the same day it is made. Does not keep well.

At left, **Peanut Wagon, H. C. Walters**
Shippensburg
c. 1900

-Shippensburg Historical Society Collection

- 1 20 ounce can pineapple chunks, drained, cut into halves
- 1 16 ounce can sliced peaches, drained, cut into halves
- 1 11 ounce can mandarin oranges, drained
- 3 medium bananas, sliced
- 2 medium apples, chopped
- 1 3¾ ounce package vanilla pudding (instant)
- 1½ cups milk
- ⅓ cup frozen orange juice concentrate, thawed
- ¾ cup sour cream

SALADS

A Delicious Salad Dressing

Makes One Half Cup

Found in the Society's "Papers of Nellie Cornman," circa 1915.

½ teaspoon dry mustard
½ teaspoon salt
1½ tablespoons sugar
1 tablespoon flour
1 dash cayenne pepper
2 egg yolks
1½ tablespoons very soft butter
1 tablespoons vinegar

Mix thoroughly the dry ingredients. Add slightly beaten egg yolks in a bowl or top of a double boiler. Stand the bowl in a sauce pan of hot water over the fire until mixture thickens. Run through a fine sieve and let stand to cool. When ready to use, if dressing is too thick, thin to desired consistency with cream or if preferred, with lemon juice.

Elizabeth Flower James

Dutch Sweet and Sour Dressing

Makes One Cup

Often found on Pennsylvania German supper tables.

1 beaten egg
¾ cup sugar
1 teaspoon cornstarch
¼ cup vinegar
⅛ cup water

Place all ingredients in a sauce pan on the stove and bring to a boil, stirring constantly for 5 to 8 minutes. Let cool and use at room temperature.

Lois Landis

Old Fashioned Cooked Salad Dressing
Makes Three Cups

This has been passed down for three generations.

Melt butter in saucepan. Add milk. When heated, stir in sugar, salt, pepper and mustard. Beat eggs and stir into mixture along with vinegar. Make paste of flour and water. Add to mixture and stir until it starts to thicken. Pour over 1 pound cooked macaroni.

Glenn E. Miller, Sr.

Note

Can also be used over cooked and cubed potatoes. Add chopped hard boiled egg and celery.

- 2 tablespoons butter or margarine
- 1 cup milk
- 2 cups sugar
- ½ teaspoon salt
- ½ teaspoon pepper
- 3 tablespoons prepared mustard
- 4 eggs
- 1 cup white vinegar
- 3 tablespoons flour

1-2-3 Dressing For Pepper Slaw
Makes Three Cups

Classic slaw dressing.

Beat first 3 ingredients for 3 minutes. Add celery seed. Will keep in the refrigerator for one month. When ready to use, grate a head of cabbage, add a little red, green or yellow pepper, chopped fine, and pour dressing over all.

Marilyn Aust

- 1 cup water
- 2 cups vinegar
- 3 cups sugar
- celery seed to taste

Dressings

Orange Salad Dressing

Makes Two Thirds Cup

Perfect for a green salad topped with mandarin oranges and red onion slices.

- ⅓ cup olive oil (not ExtraVirgin)
- 3 tablespoons raspberry vinegar
- 3 tablespoons fresh orange juice
- ½ teaspoon salt
- ⅛ teaspoon fresh ground pepper

Mix dressing ingredients and chill until ready to use.

Andrea Sheya

The Bartoli Family at their Vegetable Stand
Carlisle Farmers Market
York Road, Carlisle
c. 1960

-CCHS, Griffith Collection

Bleu Cheese Dressing

Makes Four Servings

Serve with Chicken wings, á la Boiling Springs Tavern.

Combine all ingredients, stir well. Chill. Serve with your favorite green salad.

Geoff and Debi Keith

6	ounces mayonnaise
6	ounces sour cream
⅓	cup crumbled Bleu cheese
⅓	teaspoon salt
⅛	teaspoon black pepper
⅛	teaspoon garlic powder

Medicine in Foods

The garden is a great medicine chest. Be you own doctor and look to you own slight ailments.

If you are wakeful, eat lettuce.

For infections of the skin, and yellow skin, eat onions. Onions are also good for colds, coughs, scrofula.

For a torpid liver, eat freely of asparagus.

If bowels are diseased, try blackberries.

For malaria, and general breakdown, eat cranberries.

If nervous and irritable, eat plenty of celery.

For constipation, eat fruits, ripe and healthy fruits. Fresh fruits are good. So are figs and dates. Raisins are the most beneficial.

Nellie Cornman

SALADS

ENTREES

FILET OF BEEF WITH SOUR CREAM

Serves Six

This is a beautiful, rich recipe.

1	3-pound beef tenderloin
	salt and pepper
4	tablespoons butter
1	carrot, finely chopped
1	leek, white part only, finely chopped
1	stalk celery, finely chopped

For the Sauce

1	tablespoon oil
1	clove garlic, crushed
½	pound bacon, cut into 1" pieces
¼	pound fresh mushrooms, sliced
1½	cups sour cream
2	teaspoons prepared horseradish
1	tablespoon grated onion
1	tablespoon finely chopped parsley
1	teaspoon dried thyme
1	teaspoon dried chervil

FOR THE BEEF

Preheat oven to 500°. Salt and pepper beef and dot with two tablespoons butter. In a small roasting pan, melt remaining butter and sauté carrot, leek and celery over low heat for 8 minutes. Add the beef and place in the oven for 25 minutes. Remove from oven and cool for ½ hour in pan juices, under a tent of foil.

FOR THE SAUCE

In skillet heat oil and garlic, then add bacon. Sauté until bacon is crisp and drain it on paper towels. Discard all but 3 tablespoons of fat and sauté mushrooms for 3 to 5 minutes. Drain mushrooms and set aside. Pour pan juices into bowl and add sour cream, horseradish, onion, parsley, thyme, and chervil, blending well. Add bacon bits and mushroom. Salt and pepper to taste.

TO SERVE THE BEEF

Slice filet and drizzle sauce down middle and garnish with parsley. Serve with additional dressing.

Mary Caverly

At right, **Dosh's Meat Market**
134 South East Street
Carlisle
1910

-CCHS, *Griffith Collection*

Overleaf, **Carlisle Indian and Industrial School Kitchen**
c. 1905
A. A. Line *photographer*

-CCHS

Corned Beef and Vegetable Medley

Serves Six

The vegetables add a nice change to traditional corned beef and cabbage.

Cook the corned beef by covering with water and simmer about 2 hours until fork tender. Remove beef from pot and keep warm. Add cabbage, onion, carrots, celery, potatoes, salt and pepper. Bring to boil, reduce heat and simmer covered for 30 minutes or until vegetables are tender. Arrange corned beef on a platter with vegetables and serve with the broth. A half pound of fresh broccoli may be added to simmering broth the last 5 minutes, if desired.

Joan F. Bobb

1	3 to 5 pound corned beef
1	onion studded with 3 whole cloves
6	carrots, peeled and halved
1-3	ribs of celery, halved
1	green cabbage (about 1 pound), cut into 6 wedges
6-8	small to medium potatoes
	salt and pepper to taste
½	pound fresh broccoli

Lobster Stuffed Tenderloin

Serves Six

A *perfect surf and turf dinner.*

- 3-4 pound beef tenderloin
- 2   4 ounce + frozen lobster tails
- 1 tablespoon melted butter
- 1½ teaspoons lemon juice
- 6 slices of bacon
- ½ cup sliced green onion
- ½ cup margarine
- ½ cup dry white wine
- ⅛ teaspoon garlic salt

Preheat oven to 425°. Cut tenderloin lengthwise to within ½ inch of bottom. Place frozen lobster tails in boiling salted water to cover. Simmer for 5 minutes. Remove lobster from shells. Cut tails in half lengthwise. Place lobster end to end inside beef. Combine melted margarine and lemon juice. Drizzle on lobster. Close meat around lobster and tie roast together with string. Place in roasting pan on a rack. Roast for 30 minutes. Place bacon on top of roast for 5-15 minutes longer to desired doneness. Sauté onion in margarine in sauce pan, add wine and garlic salt and heat. Slice roast and spoon on wine sauce.

Christine Deardorff

Note
The tenderloin can be stuffed and tied ahead and then refrigerated until ready to cook.

At right, **Meat Shop**
145 West Louther Street
Carlisle
c. 1910

-CCHS, Griffith Collection

Filet Mignon Superb

Serves Eight

The name says it all.

Preheat oven to 375°. Make a paste of garlic and lemon/pepper seasoning. Rub over filet. In a skillet, heat butter over medium heat until sizzling. Sear filet quickly all over until outside is crusty. Warm cognac in a small pan keeping meat in skillet with heat on, pour over meat and set aflame. When flames die out, remove filet to a large, shallow dish. Arrange mushrooms over meat. In the same skillet, melt ½ cup butter. Stir in flour. Slowly add beef broth, stirring constantly until thickened. Add steak sauce, Kitchen Bouquet, Tabasco and sherry. Blend well and simmer for 1 minute. Add salt and pepper to taste. Pour sauce over filet. Bake for 30 to 40 minutes for a large filet or 15 minutes for individual slices. Pour reserved sauce into serving bowl to accompany the meat.

Gail G. Callanan

- 3 cloves garlic, minced
- 1 teaspoon lemon/pepper seasoning
- 1 large filet (or 8 slices 1½ inch thick)
- 3 tablespoons butter
- 3 tablespoons cognac
- ¾ pound mushrooms, sliced
- ½ cup butter
- 2 tablespoons flour
- 1 cup beef broth
- 1 tablespoon steak sauce
- 1 tablespoon Kitchen Bouquet
- dash Tabasco
- ¼ cup dry sherry
- salt and fresh ground pepper

Easy Steak Diane

Serves Four

A *traditional dish made easy.*

- 1 pound beef tip or sirloin steak, ½ to ¾ inch thick
- 1 tablespoon butter or margarine
- 1 tablespoon vegetable oil
- 1 3 ounce can sliced mushrooms, drained, save broth
- 2 tablespoons butter or margarine
- 3 green onions, cleaned and sliced
- 1 teaspoon dry mustard
- 2 tablespoons lemon juice
- ½ teaspoon Worcestershire sauce
- ¼ teaspoon salt
- ¼ teaspoon pepper
- ½ teaspoon cornstarch
- ¼ teaspoon Kitchen Bouquet

Combine broth from mushrooms, mustard, lemon juice, Worcestershire sauce, salt, pepper, cornstarch and Kitchen Bouquet. Mix until smooth. Set aside. Trim fat from steak and cut into 4 serving portions. Salt and pepper meat, then quickly sear pieces in hot skillet with 1 tablespoon each of butter and vegetable oil until cooked rare. Transfer to hot serving platter and keep warm. Add remaining 2 tablespoons butter to pan drippings. Saute green onions, saving some for garnish. Add mushroom broth mixture; cook and stir until sauce thickens slightly. Add mushrooms and spoon over hot steak.

Lorraine Secrist

At right, **Beltzhoover's Food Market**
301 East Louther Street
Carlisle
1948

-CCHS, Steinmetz Collection

Grilled Flank Steak

Serves Six to Eight

Whether you use charcoal, gas or an electric grill, this is sure to be a hit.

Mix ingredients in a large plastic bag. Place steaks in bag, coating all sides. Marinade in refrigerator at least 6 hours or overnight. Place steaks on a hot grill and cook 6-7 minutes per side. Cut diagonally across the grain into ¼ inch thick slices. Serve.

Heather Kramer

- 2/3 cup Dijon mustard
- ¼ cup soy sauce
- 2 teaspoons dried thyme
- 2 teaspoons minced ginger
- ¼-½ teaspoon coarsely crushed black peppercorns
- 2 one pound flank steaks

Veal Cutlets with Spinach

Serves Four

Good with capellini aglio e olio.

- ¾ pound veal cutlets
- 1 bunch fresh spinach
- 8 ounces mushrooms
- ½ teaspoon salt
- ¼ teaspoon pepper
- flour
- butter or margarine
- ⅓ cup red wine
- ¼ teaspoon chicken flavor instant bouillon granules
- ¼ teaspoon dried thyme and/or tarragon

Pound veal cutlets until thin, and cut into medallions. Rinse spinach well and drain. Chop enough spinach to equal ½ cup; reserve remaining spinach to line platter. Slice mushrooms in half or into quarters. On waxed paper, mix salt, pepper and 3 tablespoons flour; coat veal cutlets in the flour mixture. In 12 inch skillet over medium high heat with 2 tablespoons butter or margarine, cook veal, a few pieces at a time, until browned on both sides, about 2 minutes. Remove cutlets to warm plate once brown and keep warm. Once all veal has been browned, add enough butter or margarine to drippings to sauté mushrooms, stirring frequently, until golden. In a cup, mix wine, chicken granules, dried herbs, 1 teaspoon flour and ½ cup water. Blend and add to mushrooms in skillet. Stir in chopped spinach. Over high heat, cook, stirring to loosen brown bits from bottom of skillet, until sauce boils and thickens slightly. To serve, line platter with reserved spinach leaves. Arrange cutlets on spinach and pour sauce over veal.

Lorraine Secrist

At right, **S. O. Rebok, Butcher.**
Newburg,
July 8, 1909
Clyde A. Laughlin photographer

-Shippensburg Historical Society Collection

Veal Marsala

Serves Four

Serve with pasta and a salad.

Cut scallops into two inch lengths. Unless veal is very young (almost white in color), pound it with a wooden mallet to tenderize. Cover the veal with the flour which has been seasoned with the salt and pepper. This is most easily done by mixing the flour and seasonings in a paper bag and then shaking the veal in the paper bag. Sauté the scallops in the olive oil until nicely browned. Remove scallops to a warm pan. Then sauté the onions in the olive oil in which the veal has been cooked. In a minute, add the mushrooms; then add one-half the Marsala and let it cook down. Add the parsley and the rest of the Marsala. Let it boil for one minute before pouring over the scallops.

Robert Lee Jacobs

2	pounds veal scallops
	flour
	salt and pepper
2-4	tablespoons olive oil or butter or a combination
½	cup chopped onions
1	cup sliced mushrooms
½	cup Marsala wine
1	tablespoon chopped parsley

S. O. Rebok, Butcher in Patriotic & Industrial Parade, July 3, 1909. Newburg, Pa.

Hog Maw

Serves Four to Six

 *well known central Pennsylvania dish.*

- 8 large potatoes
- 2 cups cabbage
- 1 pound fresh sausage
- 1 tablespoon salt
- 1 pig stomach, cleaned
- ¼ cup water

Preheat oven to 300°. Dice the raw potatoes, shred the cabbage. Mix the sausage, potatoes, cabbage and salt thoroughly. Stuff the pig stomach with filling. Sew up openings. Place in a roast pan with water. Cover the roast pan. Bake for 3 hours. Uncover the last hour to brown.

Bea Williams

Note
For a casserole, omit the pig stomach and water.

Grandma G's Ham Barbecue

Serves Six to Eight

 *grandmother's recipe will always be remembered as being the best.*

- 1 medium onion, chopped
- 1 green pepper, chopped
- ⅓ cup sweet pickle relish
- ⅓ cup vinegar
- ½ cup catsup
- 2 tablespoons brown sugar
- 2 pounds baked, smoked ham, chipped.

Combine all ingredients except ham. Bring to a boil. Add ham and simmer for five minutes. Serve on rolls.

Sandra Gobrecht

Note
You may want to double the sauce recipe.

Sweet Ham and Pork

Serves Six to Eight

Form into meatballs for a tangy hors d'oeuvre.

Preheat oven to 350°. Combine first 5 ingredients. Form into a loaf and place in an 8x10 glass pan. Mix together basting sauce and pour over the loaf. Baste frequently during cooking. Bake for 1½ hours.

Gail G. Callanan

1	pound ground ham
1½	pounds ground pork
2	eggs
1	cup bread crumbs
1	cup milk

Basting Sauce

½	cup vinegar
½	cup water
1½	cups brown sugar
1	tablespoon dry mustard

Peach Glazed Spareribs

Serves Six to Eight

The fresh peach glaze is also good on chicken or pork chops.

Preheat oven to 350°. Place ribs in a 5 quart pot with bay leaf and enough water to cover. Bring to a boil. Reduce heat and simmer 5 minutes. Drain spareribs and lay them on a rack in a large roasting pan. Puree peaches in a food processor until smooth. Transfer to a saucepan and bring to a boil. Stir in remaining ingredients. Roast ribs for 20 minutes. Brush with peach glaze and continue roasting for another 20 minutes, brushing frequently with the peach glaze and turning ribs occasionally.

Katy Krupp

Note
These may be barbecued over a low flame. Turn ribs frequently to avoid burning.

3	pounds pork spareribs, separated
1	bay leaf
1	pound fresh peaches, peeled, pitted and cut into chunks
1	tablespoon honey
1	teaspoon minced ginger root
1	clove garlic, minced
½	teaspoon vinegar
	dash cayenne pepper

GRILLED PORK CHOPS WITH SALAD

Serves Four

W*hich fork do you use for this one?*

For Pork Chops

- ¼ cup olive oil
- ⅛ cup red wine vinegar
- 2-3 cloves garlic, minced
- ¼ teaspoon dried thyme
- 4 one inch thick loin pork chops

For Salad

- 2 cups mixed greens, torn into small pieces, (watercress, bibb, Boston lettuce, etc.)
- 2 medium tomatoes, chopped
- ¼ cup fresh basil, minced
- ¼ cup olive oil
- ⅛ cup red wine vinegar
- 2 garlic cloves, minced
- ½ teaspoon salt
- ½ teaspoon pepper

Mix together first four ingredients for marinade. Pour marinade over pork chops and marinade for at least 2 hours, turning occasionally. Prepare grill. Combine greens with tomatoes. Blend last 6 ingredients for salad dressing. Dress salad. Grill chops over medium high heat for 10 minutes per side. Transfer chops to plate and top with salad.

Heather Kramer

Carlisle Farmers Market
York Road
c. 1960

-CCHS

Skillet Pork Chops

Serves Four

Sure to be a favorite one dish meal.

Trim fat, flour chops and brown. Combine cheese, salt and pepper and sprinkle 2 tablespoons over meat. Add potatoes in a layer and sprinkle with 1 tablespoon cheese mixture. Add a layer of onions and sprinkle with remaining cheese mixture. Dissolve bouillon in hot water and add lemon juice. Pour over meat, potatoes and onion. Simmer about 40 minutes, covered.

Shirley Halliday

Note
A deep frying pan is recommended.

- 4 pork chops or sliced tenderloin
- 2 tablespoons flour
- ⅓ cup Parmesan cheese
- ½ teaspoon salt
- ¼ teaspoon pepper
- 4 cups sliced raw potatoes
- 2 medium onions, sliced
- 3 beef bouillon cubes
- ¾ cup hot water
- 1 tablespoon lemon juice

Pork Tenderloin with Orange Sauce

Serves Four

Fabulous flavor with little effort.

Rub tenderloins with rosemary, garlic, salt and pepper. Preheat oven to 500°. Grease baking pan with oil. Bake tenderloins 18 to 20 minutes or until meat thermometer registers 155°. Transfer tenderloins to cutting board and loosely cover to keep warm. Sprinkle flour into drippings. (If there are no drippings, pour a little of the orange juice into the pan.) Place on stove top and stir over medium high heat, scraping up the brown bits. Combine orange juice and chicken broth. Slowly stir into pan; bring to a boil, stirring continually. Reduce heat and simmer 3 to 5 minutes or until slightly thickened. Slice pork, arrange on platter, drizzle a little sauce over pork. Pass remaining sauce.

Mary Finigan

- 2 small pork tenderloins, trimmed of all visible fat
- 1 teaspoon dried rosemary, crushed
- 1 teaspoon minced garlic
  salt and pepper to taste
- 1 tablespoon flour
- 1 cup orange juice
- ½ cup chicken broth

Dad's Austrian Goulash

Serves Six to Eight

Especially good on a frosty winter night.

- 2 pounds veal or chicken or pork cut into 1 inch cubes
- 2 large onions, minced
- 2 strips finely chopped bacon or 1 tablespoon fat
- 1 tablespoon paprika
- 1 teaspoon salt
- 1 tablespoon vinegar
- 1 1 pound can tomatoes, chopped
- ¼ cup water
- 1 tablespoon flour
- ½ cup sour cream

Brown onions in fat. Add meat, paprika, salt and vinegar. Cook until meat browns, stirring occasionally to prevent scorching. Add tomatoes and water. Cover and cook slowly (45 minutes) or until meat is tender, adding a little water from time to time. Taste for seasoning. Mix flour with sour cream and add to goulash. Cook for a few more minutes and serve with buttered noodles or rice.

Barbara A. McCarthy

Worldly Beef Stroganoff

Serves Four

*I*ndulge and enjoy.

Combine salt and 1 tablespoon flour; roll meat strips in mixture. Melt 2 tablespoons butter or margarine in a large skillet; add sirloin and brown on all sides. Add mushrooms, onion and garlic; cook until onion is barely tender, about 5 minutes. Remove meat and mushrooms from pan temporarily. Melt remaining butter or margarine in pan drippings and add 3 tablespoons flour, stirring to avoid lumps. Add tomato paste. Pour in consomme and cook, stirring constantly until mixture thickens. Return meat and mushrooms to skillet. Stir in sour cream and sherry; heat thoroughly, but don't boil. Serve at once over hot noodles or rice.

Gretchen Hoffman

- 1/2 teaspoon salt
- 4 tablespoons flour, divided
- 1 pound top sirloin, cut in 1/4 inch strips
- 1/4 cup butter or margarine
- 1 cup fresh sliced mushrooms
- 1/2 cup onion, chopped
- 1 clove garlic, crushed
- 1 tablespoon tomato paste
- 1 (10 1/2 oz.) can beef consomme
- 1 cup sour cream
- 2 tablespoons sherry wine
- cooked noodles or rice

At left, **Mr. David Javitch's Meat Market, now Giant Food Stores**
18 North Hanover Street
Carlisle
opened 1923

-CCHS, Collection of Joan Barnes

Braised Lamb Stew

Serves Four

This hearty dish will warm the soul.

1	tablespoon olive oil
2	pounds meaty lamb shanks
¼	cup flour
1	large onion
7	cloves garlic, peeled
2	teaspoons chopped, fresh ginger
4	medium potatoes, pared and chunked
2	large turnips, pared and chunked
3	medium carrots, pared and sliced (¼ inch)
1	cup chicken broth
½	cup dry, white wine
¾	teaspoon leaf rosemary
¾	teaspoon grated lemon rind
½	teaspoon freshly grated black pepper

Trim meat from shanks; cube. Preheat oven to 350°. Heat oil in a large ovenproof Dutch oven or pot over a moderately high heat. Dredge lamb in flour; sauté in oil until browned, about 5 minutes. Remove to plate. Lower heat. Add onion, garlic, and ginger to pot. Sauté, uncovered, until softened, about 10 minutes. Add potatoes, carrots, turnips, broth, white wine, rosemary, lemon rind, pepper and lamb. Bring to boil and cover. Bake until meat is tender, about an hour. Transfer meat and vegetables to a platter. Skim fat from sauce. Pour sauce over meat and vegetables. This dish can be prepared a day ahead and refrigerated, covered. Remove fat from surface and reheat. The flavor improves with time.

Susan Jumper

Hunter's Stew

Serves Six

The tradition of this stew goes back centuries. It was kept in well stocked larders, taken on long journeys and eaten on feast days.

Heat the oil in a large, flameproof casserole. Slice onion thickly and add with the garlic and cook 2 to 3 minutes. Remove and set aside. Add the meat in four small batches, cooking over high heat to brown. When all the meat is browned, return it to the casserole with the onions and garlic. Sprinkle over the flour and cook until light brown. Add paprika and cook 1 to 2 minutes, stirring constantly. Pour on the stock gradually and bring to the boil. Turn down the heat to simmering and add the smoked meats, herbs, salt, pepper, cayenne and tomato puree. Stir well, cover and cook over low heat for 45 minutes. Stir occasionally and add more liquid if necessary during cooking. When the meat is almost tender, add cabbage, apples, carrots, and prunes. Cook an additional 20 minutes. Add the tomatoes, wine or Madeira and a pinch of sugar, if desired. Cook 10 minutes more. Adjust the seasoning and serve immediately.

Maxim Dem'Chak

At left, **Hunting Scene**
Shippensburg
1937

-CCHS

4	tablespoons oil
1	pound stewing steak, pork, or venison cut into 2 inch pieces
1	onion
2	cloves garlic, crushed
4	tablespoons flour
2	tablespoons mild paprika
4	cups light stock
4	ounces smoked ham, cut in 2 inch pieces
4	ounces smoked sausage, cut into 2 inch pieces
1	teaspoon marjoram
1	teaspoon chopped parsley
	salt and pepper
	pinch cayenne pepper
2	tablespoons tomato paste
1	head white cabbage, chopped
2	apples, cored and chopped
2	carrots, thinly sliced
8	pitted prunes, roughly chopped
3	tomatoes, peeled and roughly chopped
1/3	cup red wine or Madeira
	pinch of sugar

Meat

Cashew Chicken

Serves Four

T*he marinade is versatile: adapt this recipe to the vegetables on hand.*

- 2 chicken breasts, skinned, boned and cut into 1-inch strips
- 2 tablespoons soy sauce
- 2 tablespoons rice wine or sherry
- 2 teaspoons corn starch
- 1/8 teaspoon pepper
- 4 tablespoons vegetable or peanut oil, divided
- 2 stalks celery, thinly sliced
- 1/2 cup bamboo shoots
- 1/2 cup sliced water chestnuts
- 1/4 pound snow peas, ends snipped
- 1 clove garlic, minced
- 2 green onions, chopped including green part
- 1 cup cashews
  cooked rice

Put chicken in a small bowl. Add the soy sauce, rice wine or sherry, corn starch and pepper. Stir well. Let marinate for at least 30 minutes. Heat 2 tablespoons of the oil in a wok or large frying pan. Add the celery and stir fry for two minutes. Add the bamboo shoots, water chestnuts and snow peas and stir fry for another minute or two. Remove to a large bowl and keep warm. Don't cook very long; everything is meant to be crunchy. Add the remaining two tablespoons of oil to the wok. Add the garlic and green onion. Stir fry for 30 seconds. Add the chicken and its marinade and stir fry for 2 to 3 minutes or until cooked through. Add the cashews and stir fry for one minute longer. Mix the vegetables with the chicken and cashews. Serve with rice.

Gretchen Hoffman

American Hotel, Mechanicsburg, Pa.

CURRIED CHICKEN BREASTS

Serves Four

Indian Rice and sliced cucumbers make a nice accompaniment to this dish.

Heat 1 tablespoon of the butter in a saucepan. Add onion, garlic, apple and celery. Stir until wilted. Add curry powder, stir. Add tomatoes, chicken broth, bay leaf, salt and pepper. Bring to a boil and simmer for 15 minutes, stirring often. Discard bay leaf and put mixture through a food processor or food mill and process to a fine texture. Sprinkle chicken with salt and pepper. Heat remaining butter in a nonstick skillet and add chicken. Cook over moderate heat until lightly browned. Turn pieces and cook about 5 minutes more. Do not overcook. Pour sauce over chicken, bring to a boil and simmer for 5 minutes. Sprinkle with chopped coriander and serve.

Katy Krupp

- 3 tablespoons butter
- ½ cup chopped onions
- 2 teaspoons chopped garlic
- 1 apple, cored and finely cubed, about 1 cup
- ½ cup finely chopped celery
- 2 tablespoons curry powder
- ½ cup canned crushed tomatoes
- ¾ cup chicken broth, fresh or canned
- 1 bay leaf
  salt and pepper to taste
- 4 skinless, boneless chicken breast halves, about 1¼ pound total
- 4 tablespoons coarsely chopped coriander

These are my banties taken in 1906.

Postcard from Fanny Andrews

-CCHS

At far left, **American Hotel,**
W. Hiller proprietor
6 North Market Street
Mechanicsburg
c. 1910

-CCHS

Orange Honey Mustard Chicken

Serves Four

Easy preparation produces a wonderful flavor.

- 1 pound skinless, boneless chicken breasts
- 4 teaspoons olive oil
- ½ cup minced shallots
- 2 cloves garlic, minced
- 1 cup fresh orange juice
- Grated rind of two oranges
- 1 tablespoon honey mustard
- ground pepper

Wash and dry chicken breasts and cut in thirds. Saute in 2 teaspoons hot oil in nonstick pan until brown on both sides. Set aside. Add remaining oil and sauté shallots and garlic in oil until shallots begin to brown. Stir in orange juice, rind, honey mustard and pepper to taste. Reduce heat and return chicken to pan. Cover and simmer about 5 to 7 minutes, until chicken is cooked through. Serve topped with sauce.

Andrea Sheya

Retrieving Bees
c. 1920
-CCHS

MEXICAN CHICKEN KIEV

Serves Eight

This entree can be refrigerated overnight, or frozen, to bake later.

Wash and dry chicken breasts. Pound thin. Divide green chilies in eighths and with one strip jack cheese in center of each chicken breast; roll up and tuck ends under. Combine last 6 ingredients. Dip chicken in melted butter and roll in crumb mixture. Place seam side down in casserole, drizzle with any remaining butter. Cover and chill for 4 hours or overnight. (If freezing, freeze at this point and defrost before baking.) Preheat oven to 400°, and bake, uncovered, for 20-25 minutes.

Susan Dossett

Note
Serve with sour cream and salsa if desired.

- 8 chicken breast halves, boned, skinned
- 1 7 ounce can diced green chilies
- ¼ pound Monterey Jack cheese, cut into 8 strips
- 6 tablespoons melted butter or margarine
- ½ cup Italian bread crumbs
- ¼ cup Parmesan cheese
- 1 tablespoon chili powder
- ½ teaspoon salt
- ¼ teaspoon ground cumin
- ¼ teaspoon pepper

CHICKEN PARMESAN

Serves Four

Looking for a healthy dish, use fat free mayonnaise.

Preheat oven to 325°. In a flat bowl, whisk mayonnaise and water together until smooth. In another flat bowl, mix parmesan cheese, bread crumbs and parsley flakes. Dip flattened chicken in mayonnaise mixture, then in cheese and bread crumb mixture until coated generously. Place on ungreased baking sheet. Bake for 30 minutes covered with aluminum foil. Remove foil and bake an additional 30 minutes uncovered.

Eileen Swidler

- 4 chicken breasts or thighs, boneless and skinless and pounded to ¾-inch thick
- ¾ cup grated Parmesan cheese
- ¼ cup bread crumbs
- 1 tablespoon parsley flakes
- ½ cup mayonnaise (low fat or regular)
- ¼ cup water

BILL WASHINGTON'S CHICKEN SOUFFLE

Serves Eight to Ten

Bill was a familiar sight at the President's home on the campus of Dickinson College, as well as other homes in Carlisle.

- 8 slices bread, crusts removed (use crusts for crumbs)
- 4 cups cooked chicken, cubed
- ½ pound mushrooms, sliced or 3 ounce can
- 1 cup water chestnuts, drained and sliced thin (8 oz. can)
- 6 slices processed cheese
- 2 cups milk
- 4 eggs
- salt to taste
- 1 can mushroom soup
- 1 can celery soup
- 1 jar chopped pimento
- ¼ cup butter
- ½ cup mayonnaise
- 2 cups buttered crumbs

Line a large shallow buttered 3 quart casserole with bread slices. Top with cooked chicken. Cook mushrooms 5 minutes, spoon over chicken. Add water chestnuts. Dot with mayonnaise and top with cheese. Combine eggs with milk and salt. Pour over chicken mixture. Mix soups and pimento and spoon over. Refrigerate overnight. Cover with foil and bake at 350° for 1½ hours. Remove foil the last 15 minutes and top with buttered crumbs.

Elaine Faller

Hollar Building Tea Room and Banquet Hall
50th Anniversary Dinner of Cumberland Valley Hose Company Shippensburg 1909

-Shippensburg Historical Society Collection

Chicken Lasagna

Serves Twelve

A recipe for lasagna lovers who love chicken.

Preheat oven to 350°. To prepare the sauce, melt butter, sauté vegetables and stir in soup and milk. Cook noodles and drain. Place half of the noodles in buttered baking dish. Cover noodles with one half of the mushroom sauce, ricotta, chicken, cheddar and Parmesan cheeses. Repeat with the other half. Bake for 45 minutes.

Jill Bream

8	ounces lasagna noodles
1½	cups ricotta or cottage cheese
3	cups chopped cooked chicken
2	cups grated cheddar cheese
½	cup Parmesan cheese

For the Mushroom Sauce

3	tablespoons butter
½	cup chopped onion
2	cloves garlic, minced
½	cup chopped green pepper
3	cans cream of mushroom or chicken soup
¾	cup milk
1	6 ounce can of sliced mushrooms
½	teaspoon basil

Dining Room at Lindner Estate
Forest Hills Bungalow
c. 1920
A. A. Line photographer

-CCHS

Amaretto Chicken

Serves Twelve

Perk up palates with this almond flavored chicken.

Preheat oven to 350°. Mix flour, salt and paprika on aluminum foil. Dredge chicken in flour mixture and brown lightly in a skillet with butter. Add water to skillet. Simmer 30 minutes. Arrange chicken in 9x13 dish. Mix cornstarch in half and half. Add Amaretto, lemon peel and lemon juice. Cook until sauce has thickened. Pour over chicken. (At this point this dish may be frozen.) Bake chicken, covered, for 35 minutes. Remove the cover and sprinkle with cheese. Bake until cheese melts.

Kathy Noaker

¼	cup flour
2½	teaspoons salt
1	teaspoon paprika
6	whole chicken breasts, halved, boned and skinned
¼	cup butter
¼	cup water
2	teaspoons corn starch
1	cup half and half
¼	to ½ cup Amaretto liqueur
1	teaspoon lemon peel
1	tablespoon lemon juice
1	cup grated Swiss cheese

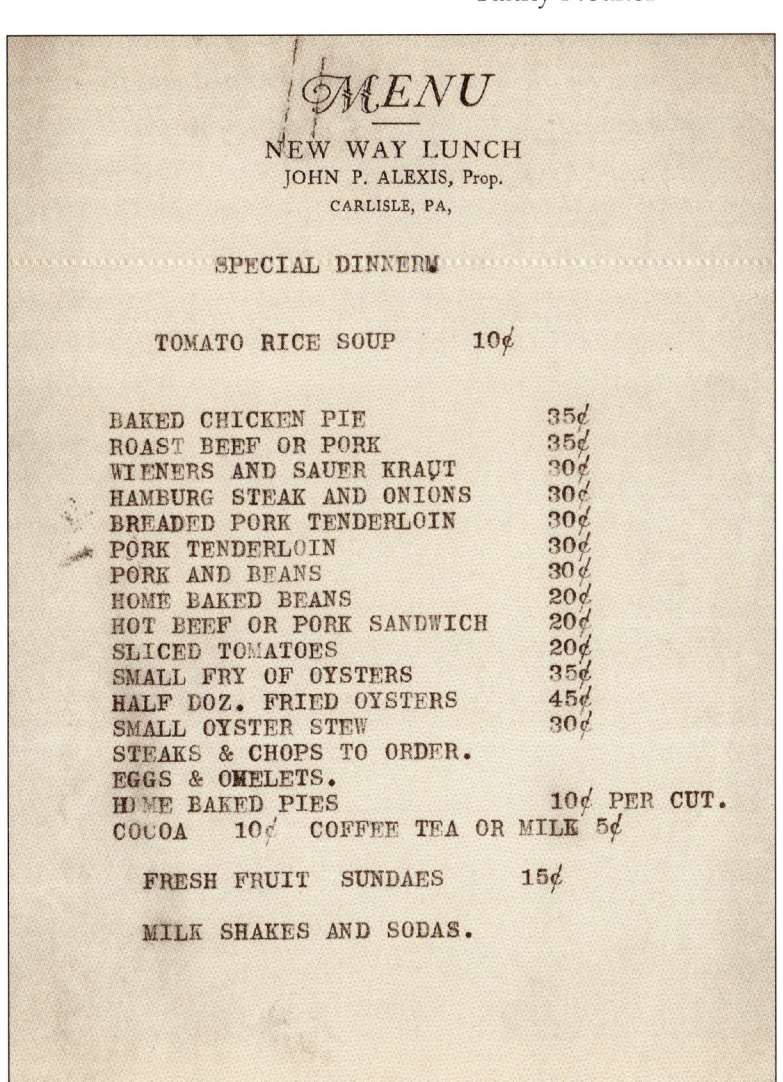

New Way Restaurant
Lunch Menu
1930

-CCHS

Noakers Market
Corner of A and Pitt Streets
Carlisle
1957

-CCHS

Fancy Chicken Pot Pie

Serves Six

Milk and/or chicken broth may be substituted for the cream, but the tarragon is essential.

For the Crust

- 1½ cups sifted flour
- ½ teaspoon salt
- 1 stick cold butter, cut in small pieces
- ¼ cup ice water

For the Pot Pie

- 4 whole skinless chicken breasts (2 pounds)
- 1 cup heavy cream
- 4 carrots, peeled and cut into ½ inch pieces
- 2 zucchini, unpeeled, cut into ½ inch pieces
- 5 tablespoons butter
- 2 small yellow onions, coarsely chopped
- 5 tablespoons flour
- 1 cup chicken broth
- ¼ cup Cognac or white wine
- 1 tablespoon dried tarragon
- 1½ teaspoons salt
- ½ teaspoon pepper
- 1 egg
- 1 tablespoon water

To Make the Crust in a Food Processor

Process the flour and salt with a steel blade just to mix. Add the butter and pulse until the mixture resembles coarse meal. With the machine running, add the ice water and process until the dough leaves the side of the bowl. Turn the dough out onto a lightly floured surface, shape into a thick circle, and wrap in plastic. Refrigerate at least 30 minutes before using.

To Make the Pot Pie

Preheat oven to 350°. Place the chicken in a single layer in a baking pan. Pour cream over and bake for 20 to 25 minutes. Remove the chicken from the cream; reserve the cream and cooking juices. Let the chicken cool and cut into 1 inch pieces. Blanch the carrots in boiling salted water for 3 minutes. Add the zucchini and cook 1 minute more. Cool under cold running water. Drain thoroughly. *May be made ahead to this point.* Melt the butter in a large pan over medium heat. Add the onions and sauté until translucent, about 5 minutes. Add the flour and cook, stirring constantly, for 5 minutes. Do not let the flour brown. Add the broth and cook, stirring constantly, until thickened. Stir in reserved cream, cooking juices and wine. Cook over low heat until thick, about 5 minutes. Stir in the tarragon, salt, and pepper and simmer 1 minute. Add the chicken and vegetables and mix gently into the cream sauce. Remove from the heat. Preheat oven to 425°. Mix the egg and water in a small bowl. Pour the chicken filling into a deep 2 quart casserole or soufflé dish. Roll out the pastry and place on the dish, leaving a 1 inch border. Brush the top with the egg wash. Cut a steam vent in the center. Place the dish on a baking sheet and bake at 425° for 20 to 25 minutes.

Susan D'Lamater

Crab Maryland

Serves Four

An elegant dish, perfect when crab is plentiful.

- 1 pound backfin lump crab meat, picked
- 1 cup chopped celery
- ⅔ cup mayonnaise or salad dressing
- ¼ cup milk
- ¼ cup chopped onion
- 1 teaspoon Worcestershire sauce
- ½ teaspoon salt, dash pepper
- 1½ cups soft bread crumbs
- 2 tablespoons butter or margarine, melted

Preheat oven to 350°. Combine seafood with next 6 ingredients. Spoon into 1 quart casserole or 4 individual baking shells. Combine 1 cup crumbs and melted butter. Sprinkle around edge of casserole. Bake, uncovered, until heated through, 30-35 minutes for casserole and 20-25 minutes for shells.

Helen Ashway

Inside menu
Julius Restaurant
49 West Main Street
Carlisle
1930

-CCHS

MENU

RELISHES

Table Celery	.15	Sweet Pickles	.15
Head Lettuce	.15	Dill Pickles	.10
Cold Slaw	.10	Stuffed Olives	.15

SOUPS

Chicken	.15	Vegetable	.10
Tomato	.10	Clam Chowder	.15

With Bread and Butter 5c Extra

STEAKS, CHOPS, ETC.

The Following Orders Include Bread, Butter and Home Fried Potatoes

Small Steak	.50	Lamb Chops	.50
Small Steak with Onions	.60	Pork Chops	.50
Small Steak with Mushrooms	.70	Pork Sausage	.40
Sirloin Steak	.60	Pork Sausage with Cakes	.40
Sirloin Steak with Onions	.70	Hamburger Steak	.30
Sirloin Steak with Mushrooms	.80	Hamburger Steak with Onions	.40
Porterhouse Steak	.75	Fried Ham	.40
Veal Steak	.50	Fried Bacon	.40
Veal Chops	.50	Veal Cutlets, Breaded	.40

Baked Beans	.20
Ham and Beans	.30
Side Dish of Beans	.10

EGGS AND OMELETTES

The Following Orders Include Bread, Butter and Home Fried Potatoes

Ham and Eggs and Potatoes	.45	Chicken Omelette	.45
Bacon and Eggs and Potatoes	.45	Tomato Omelette and Potatoes	.40
Plain Omelette	.25	Jelly Omelette	.40
Oyster Omelette	.40	Onion Omelette and Potatoes	.40
Cheese Omelette and Potatoes	.40	Spanish Omelette and Potatoes	.45
Ham Omelette and Potatoes	.40	Mushroom Omelette	.50
Two Eggs, Fried	.25	Two Poached Eggs, Plain	.25
Two Eggs, Boiled	.25	Two Poached Eggs on Toast	.30

Two Eggs, Scrambled .25

OYSTERS IN SEASON

One Dozen Raw	.45	One-half Dozen Fried	.40
One-half Dozen Raw	.25	One Dozen Stewed	.55
One Dozen Fried	.75	One-half Dozen Stewed	.30

If Satisfied Tell Others—If Not Tell Us

Crab Cakes

Serves Four to Six

Make these even more delectable with lump crab meat.

Beat eggs with mayonnaise, mustard, parsley, Old Bay (if using) and bread. Stir in crab meat. Mix until ready, adding crumbs, if needed. Press into patties and brown on both sides in a medium-hot, greased skillet.

Sarah Haddock Masland

- 1 egg
- 2 tablespoons mayonnaise
- 1 tablespoon Dijon mustard
- 1/4 cup minced parsley
- 4 slices white bread, trimmed of crusts and cubed
- 1 pound lump crab meat, picked over
- bread crumbs
- butter for pan
- 2 teaspoons Old Bay, optional

Baked Seafood Supreme

Serves Four

Simple and elegant.

Preheat oven to 400°. Mix all ingredients together, except bread crumbs. Turn into a 1½ quart casserole dish. Top with the bread crumbs. Bake uncovered for 20 minutes.

Sheila Highlands

- 1 pound crabmeat
- 1 cup mayonnaise
- 1/2 cup green pepper, finely chopped
- 1 teaspoon salt
- 1 pound shrimp, cooked and peeled
- 1/2 cup celery, finely chopped
- 1/4 cup onion, minced
- 2 cups buttered bread crumbs

Stromboli

Serves Three to Four

Super *Sunday evening supper.*

- 1 loaf frozen bread dough, thawed
- ½-1 pound chopped ham
- 2 cups shredded mozzarella cheese
- 2 egg whites, optional
- 2 tablespoons oil
- ¼ teaspoon pepper
- 1 teaspoon oregano
- 2 tablespoons Parmesan cheese
- ½ teaspoon garlic powder
- 1 teaspoon parsley flakes

Preheat oven to 350°. Roll and pull thawed bread dough to 9x13 inch size. Mix last 6 ingredients together and spread like butter over bread dough. Top with ham and cheese. Roll dough like a jelly roll and crease top. Turn over so crease is on the bottom. Place on a cookie sheet. Brush top with egg white. Bake for 30 to 40 minutes.

Pat Simms

Lisburn Lasagna

Serves Twelve

In a hurry, substitute a jar of spagetti sauce.

Preheat oven to 350°. For a pan that takes 12 whole lasagna noodles in 3 layers of 4 noodles each:
Heat water, oil and oregano to boiling in a large pot while cooking sauce. Split casings of sausage, crumble meat and sauté with onion and garlic (to taste). Add tomatoes, paste, herbs and wine. Simmer, covered. Cook noodles to package directions, adding olive oil and oregano to water. Grease pan lightly. Keep noodles in pot while assembling (therefore turn off heat before too soft). Alternate layers of noodles, 4 or 5 spoonfuls of ricotta, ⅓ of the cooked meat sauce and slices of mozzarella. Repeat twice, sprinkle Parmesan on top of last mozzarella layer. Bake for 20 minutes.

Virginia A. LaFond

Note
May be prepared ahead of time and baked just before serving.

12	lasagna noodles,
	water
	olive oil
	oregano
1	pound Italian sausage (½ hot and ½ sweet - can be adjusted)
	chopped onion
	minced garlic
2-3	cans (14 ounce) of tomatoes
1	can tomato paste
	rosemary
	thyme
	oregano
½	cup red wine (dry)
3	8 ounce packs of mozzarella cheese, sliced
1	pound Ricotta cheese
⅓	cup Parmesan cheese, grated

At left, **Butchering**
Rural Cumberland County
c. 1920

-Shippensburg Historical Society Collection

PASTA

Penne with Red Pepper Sauce

Serves Four to Six

Nouveau pasta.

olive oil
6 halves sun-dried tomatoes, chopped
3 large cloves garlic, minced
1 large onion, in thin slivers
4 large red bell peppers, julienned
1/8 teaspoon red pepper flakes
1 tablespoon balsamic vinegar
  salt and pepper to taste
6 large basil leaves chopped
2-3 tablespoons sour cream
8 ounces cooked penne pasta
  Parmesan cheese

In a large skillet, heat olive oil and add sun-dried tomatoes, garlic, onion, bell peppers and red pepper flakes. Cook for 10 minutes. Stir in balsamic vinegar, salt and pepper, basil leaves and sour cream. Serve over cooked penne pasta. Garnish with grated Parmesan cheese.

Pam Merlie

Ivo Otto Farm
South Middleton Township
-CCHS

Sour Cream Enchiladas

Serves Six

Add *cooked shredded chicken breasts for a more substantial dish.*

Preheat oven to 350°. In a large bowl, blend the first 6 ingredients. Beat until smooth. In a heavy skillet, heat oil and holding tortillas with tongs, dip in hot oil for a few seconds on each side. Tortillas should be limp. Drain tortillas on paper towels. Place 1 strip cheese in center of each tortilla. Add 1-2 teaspoons of green chilies and 1 large tablespoon of cream mixture. Roll tortillas and place seam side down in a 9x13 inch casserole. Cover with remaining cream mixture and chopped scallions. Bake 30 minutes.

Andrea Sheya

Note
Low fat or no fat cottage cheese, cream cheese and sour cream may be substituted.

- 1 pint cottage cheese
- 2 8 ounce packages of cream cheese
- 1 pint sour cream
- 1 clove of garlic, crushed
- 1 teaspoon salt
- 4 ounces green chili salsa
- ½ cup oil
- 12 corn tortillas
- 1 pound Monterey Jack cheese, cut into 12 finger sized strips
- 1 4 ounce can diced green chilies

VEGETABLES

GREENS WITH GARLIC, RAISINS & PINE NUTS

Serves Four to Six

Any hardy green may be used; spinach is a good substitute.

- 1½-2 pounds broccoli rabe
- 3 tablespoons olive oil
- 2 large cloves garlic, minced
- ½ cup pine nuts, lightly toasted
- ¼ cup raisins
- 2 tablespoons balsamic vinegar
- ½ teaspoon salt
- 1 small red onion, shredded finely

Bring ⅓ cup water to boil in a non reactive pan, and add greens gradually. When wilted, partially cover and reduce heat, stirring occasionally, until greens are soft but not falling apart, about 15 minutes for broccoli rabe and 5 minutes for spinach. There should be almost no liquid left. If necessary, remove greens and boil liquid until reduced to a few tablespoons and return greens to pan. While greens are cooking, combine oil and garlic in small skillet, cook over medium low heat, 3 to 4 minutes, until garlic is softened but not brown. Stir in the pine nuts and raisins and set aside. When greens are done, stir in vinegar and salt and then the oil mixture. Garnish with shredded onion.

Frances Decker

Overleaf, **Carlisle Market House on the Square**
c. 1930
-CCHS

At right, **Sauerkraut Wagon**
Shippensburg
c. 1910
-Shippensburg Historical Society Collection

Crumbly Green Beans

Serves Eight

Great for those Cumberland County covered dish suppers.

Preheat oven to 400°. Mix corn flakes crumbs and melted butter. Set aside. Melt 2 tablespoons butter, add flour and cook 1 to 2 minutes over low/medium heat. Add salt, pepper, sugar and onion powder. Add sour cream gradually, stirring until thick and creamy. Gently fold in beans; heat thoroughly. Pour into a 1½ quart oblong baking dish. Cover with grated cheese, then with buttered crumbs. Bake for 20 minutes.

Edna Kadel

- 1 cup corn flakes crumbs
- 2 tablespoons melted butter
- 2 tablespoons butter
- 2 tablespoons flour
- ¼ teaspoon salt
- ¼ teaspoon pepper
- 1 teaspoon sugar
- ⅛ teaspoon onion powder
- 1 cup sour cream
- 2 15 ounce cans french style green beans, drained
- 8 ounces grated Swiss cheese

Potato Filling

Serves Six

Y*ou can stuff a fowl, fill a casserole or just brown in a skillet.*

- 1 cup mashed potatoes
- 2 beaten eggs
- 4 slices of bread
- 1 cup milk
- 2 tablespoons butter
- 2 tablespoons chopped onion
- 1 tablespoon parsley
- salt and pepper to taste

Preheat oven to 375°. With a fork, mix eggs and potatoes. Break the bread into pieces and mix with the potato mixture. Pour milk over mixture to soak. Brown onions in butter. Stir onions and seasonings into filling. Spoon into a greased casserole and bake for one hour.

Bea Williams

Moore Hash Browns

Serves Four

This recipe is adapted from the 21 Club in New York, and when served in our home, the guests always ask for Moore!

Peel potatoes and cut into ½ inch cubes. There should be about 3 cups. In a large pan of boiling salted water parboil 5 minutes. Drain and cool. In a skillet, heat oil and 1 tablespoon butter until hot but not smoking and saute onions and red pepper, stirring occasionally, until soft and caramelized. Cool onions and red pepper, and in a bowl combine with potatoes, stirring vigorously to partially break up potatoes. (At this point, they may be prepared up to one day ahead and chilled.) Preheat oven to 350°. In a 10 inch non stick skillet, heat remaining two tablespoons butter over moderate heat until foam subsides and cook potato mixture, packing it evenly in skillet with back of spatula to form a cake, until underside is golden, about 10 minutes. Invert cookie sheet with out sides over skillet and carefully invert potato cake onto it. Carefully slide potato cake back into skillet and brown other side. On baking sheet or in skillet, bake potato cake 10 minutes. Sprinkle cake with salt and pepper and serve in wedges.

James P. Sheya

- 1½ pounds baking potatoes
- ¼ cup vegetable oil
- 3 tablespoons butter
- 1½ large onions, cut into ½ inch dice
- 1 bunch scallions, chopped
- ½ red pepper, diced
- fresh ground pepper and salt to taste

At left, **Carlisle Market House on the Square**
c. 1920

-CCHS

APPLE-ORANGE SWEET POTATO GALETTE

Serves Six

An interesting and wonderful combination.

- 2 medium seedless oranges, peeled and sliced
- 2 teaspoons grated orange rind
- 4 medium sweet potatoes, peeled and sliced
- 2 medium apples, peeled, cored, and sliced
- ½ cup sugar
- ½ cup brown sugar
- 1 teaspoon allspice
- 2 tablespoons butter, melted

Preheat oven to 325°. Boil sweet potatoes approximately 5 minutes. Grease a 2 quart casserole. Mix together sugar, brown sugar, allspice, orange rind and melted butter. Alternate potatoes, apples, and orange slices with the mixed ingredients. Bake for 30 to 40 minutes.

Frances Freet

VEGETABLE COUSCOUS

Serves Four

Try it, you'll like it.

- 1½ tablespoons butter
- 3 spring onions, sliced
- 2 garlic cloves, minced
- ½ red bell pepper, julienned
- ¼ pound sugar peas, julienned
- ⅛ cup golden raisins
- 1½ cups chicken broth
- 2 tablespoons fresh basil, chopped
- 1 tablespoon parsley, chopped
- salt and pepper to taste
- 1 cup couscous

In a large skillet, sauté vegetables and raisins in butter until crisp-tender, about 5 minutes. Add boiling chicken broth, herbs, salt, pepper and couscous. Remove from heat, cover and let stand 10 minutes. Fluff with a fork.

Anne Pass

Indian Rice

Serves Four

Good with any chicken dish.

In a heavy saucepan with a tight fitting lid, melt 1 tablespoon of the butter and add onions. Cook, stirring, until wilted. Add rice and cook, stirring about 30 seconds. Add broth, raisins, lemon rind, bay leaf, saffron, Tabasco, salt and pepper. Bring to a boil. Simmer over low heat for 17 minutes. Uncover and remove bay leaf. Add remaining butter and stir to fluff the rice well.

Katy Krupp

- 2 tablespoons butter
- ¼ cup finely chopped onions
- 1 cup converted rice
- 1½ cups fresh or canned chicken broth
- ¼ cup golden raisins
- 1 teaspoon grated lemon rind
- 1 bay leaf
- ½ teaspoon stem saffron
- ¼ teaspoon Tabasco
- salt and pepper to taste

Seasoned Onion Rice

Serves Six

Company rice, no last minute fuss.

Preheat oven to 350°. Coat medium saucepan with cooking spray; add onion and sauté 5 minutes. Add remaining ingredients and bring to a boil. Coat a 1½ quart casserole with cooking spray; add rice mixture. Cover and bake at 350° for 1 hour.

Caren LaRue

- 1 medium onion, finely chopped
- 1 cup uncooked white rice
- 1 (10¾ ounce) can chicken broth, undiluted
- ¾ cup water
- 1 tablespoon Worcestershire sauce
- 1 beef flavored bouillon cube
- ¼ teaspoon pepper

PENNSYLVANIA POWER & LIGHT COMPANY
GAS COOKING SCHOOL

Under Direction of

MR. C. K. STEINMETZ, District Manager, MISS EDNA MOHR and MISS PAULINE BLAINE

THURSDAY, FEBRUARY 15th, 1934

OVEN MEAL
Baked Halibut Steak
Duchess Potatoes
Escalloped Tomatoes
Stuffed Onions with Pecan Meats
Fluffy Bread Pudding

SURFACE MEAL
Spanish Lima Beans

Orange Nut Cake
Lemon Meringue Pie
Surprise Sponge Cake
Pastel Frosting
Peppermint Mousse—Chocolate Sauce
Apple Waffles

BAKED HALIBUT STEAK

Halibut Steak, 2 inches thick. Place on well-greased pan, sprinkle with salt and pepper and dot with butter. Place in a cold oven, set adjustable pointer at 325 degrees and bake 1¼ hours. Serve with tomato sauce.

DUCHESS POTATOES

2 cups hot mashed potatoes   ½ teaspoon salt
2 tablespoons butter   1 egg yolk slightly beaten

To the potatoes add the butter, salt and egg yolk. Shape, using pastry bag and tube, sprinkle with paprika. These can also be brushed over with beaten egg diluted with one teaspoon water and browned in a hot oven.

ESCALLOPED TOMATOES

Drain one can of whole tomatoes. Pour into a baking dish with a small amount of juice. Season with sugar, salt and pepper. Down through the tomatoes pack soft bread crumbs until the tomaoes and crumbs are tightly packed. Cover with buttered crumbs and bake with oven meal.

STUFFED ONIONS

4 Spanish onions   ½ cup medium white sauce
½ cup dry bread crumbs   ½ cup nuts
¼ teaspoon salt   1 beaten egg yolk
½ teaspoon chopped parsley 2 teaspoons butter

Peel onions. Steam whole until almost tender. When cool, cut out center of onion from root end, leaving shell of onion. Chop the onion removed from center, add chopped nuts, other ingredients and stuff the shell. Cover with buttered crumbs and sprinkle with paprika. Place in a baking dish and bake with oven meal. Onions can also be filled with buttered seasoned bread crumbs and sprinkled with grated cheese, if desired.

FLUFFY BREAD PUDDING

2 cups soft bread crumbs   3 eggs slightly beaten
3 cups milk, scalded   ½ teaspoon salt
¼ cup sugar   1 teaspoon vanilla
3 tablespoons butter   ½ cup seedless raisins
                            marshmallows

Soak crumbs in scalded milk. When cooled add sugar, butter, eggs, salt, flavoring and raisins. Line bottom of greased pan or casserole with marshmallows, pour mixture over marshmallows and bake with oven meal.

SURFACE MEAL

SPANISH LIMA BEANS

1 lb. ground beef   ⅛ teaspoon pepper
1 onion chopped   1 teaspoon Worcestershire sauce
1 green pepper chopped   2 cups lima beans (left over
2 tablespoons butter   cooked beans or canned)
2 cups strained tomatoes   ½ cup grated American cheese
½ teaspoon salt

Brown meat, onion and pepper in butter. Season. Add other ingredients—cover and cook about 45 minutes, using a very low flame.

ORANGE NUT CAKE

½ cup shortening   2 cups sifted flour
1 cup sugar   1 teaspoon soda
2 eggs   ½ cup nut meats
¾ cup sour cream   1 tablespoon grated orange rind

Cream the shortening—gradually add the sugar and cream well. Add beaten eggs. Sift the soda with the sifted flour and add alternately with the sour cream. Add nut meats and grated rind. Pour into a greased pan and bake at 375 degrees 25 to 30 minutes. While the cake is hot and still in the pan, pour and spread over the top of the cake ½ cup of orange juice that has been mixed with ½ cup of sugar and 1 teaspoon of orange rind. This in no way spoils the cake. Cut in squares and serve.

LEMON MERINGUE PIE

1 cup sugar   ½ teaspoon salt
1½ cups boiling water   1/3 cup lemon juice
3 tablespoons cornstarch   grated rind of 1 lemon
3 tablespoons flour   3 egg yolks

Mix dry ingredients. Add boiling water. Cook over low heat until thick. Add beaten egg yolks and cook 2 minutes longer. Add lemon juice and rind. Cool and pour into baked pie shell, cover with meringue.

MERINGUE

3 egg whites   6 tablespoons sugar

Beat the whites until stiff, add sugar gradually and beat until creamy. Pile on top of pie and brown in oven at 325 degrees 15 to 20 mniutes.

SURPRISE SPONGE CAKE

Separate 6 eggs. To the yolks add ½ cup of cold water and beat well. Add gradually 1½ cups of sugar, beating until sugar is thoroughly dissolved. Add 2 cups of flour and 2 teaspoons of baking powder sifted together. Lastly, fold in the stiffly beaten egg whites with ½ teaspoon lemon extract. Pour into large ungreased tube pan. Preheat oven to 325 degrees and bake 1 hour. When baked invert pan and allow to cool. When cool, cut cake in half, spread between the layers with pastel frosting and sprinkle with cocoanut. Spread outside of cake with frosting and sprinkle well with cocoanut.

PASTEL FROSTING

½ cup jelly (any tart flavor)
1 egg white unbeaten
dash of salt

Place jelly in a bowl over hot water. Add egg white and salt and beat with rotary beater until jelly is free from lumps. Remove from range and continue beating until mixture is stiff enough to stand in peaks. Spread on cake. Garnish with bits of clear jelly and serve at once.

PEPPERMINT MOUSSE

1 teaspoon gelatin   1 cup cream
2 tablespoons cold water   ⅛ teaspoon salt
1 cup milk   1 teaspoon vanilla
            ½ cup crushed cream mint candies

Soak gelatin in cold water about five minutes. Heat milk and dissolve gelatin in it. Add crushed candies and salt. Cool and add flavoring. Turn into freezing tray, when mixture begins to thicken turn into bowl and beat until frothy. Then fold in stiffly beaten cream, and a few drops of green vegetable coloring. Mix well. Pour into refrigerator tray and freeze without stirring. Garnish with pistachio nuts or serve with Chocolate Sauce.

CHOCOLATE SAUCE

1 square Baker's unsweetened   4 tablespoons sugar
    chocolate, cut in pieces   dash of salt
3 tablespoons water   few drops vanilla
1½ tablespoons melted butter

Combine chocolate, water, sugar, and salt in double boiler. Heat and blend. Add butter and vanilla. Beat well. Makes 2/3 cup.

APPLE WAFFLES

1½ cups flour   1 cup milk
2 teaspoons baking powder   6 tablespoons melted butter
½ teaspoon salt   1 tablespoon sugar
2 eggs   1¾ cups chopped apples
1/3 teaspoon cinnamon

Sift dry ingredients together, add the beaten egg yolks with the milk. Beat until smooth, then add chopped apple. Add melted butter and fold in stiffly beaten egg whites. This recipe makes six waffles.

Mushroom & Arugula Risotto

Serves Twelve

Check the Lemoyne Farmer's Market for Reggiano-Parmigiano. It has a special flavor, but you may substitute freshly grated Parmesan.

FOR PORCHINI BROTH:

Rinse the dirt from the mushrooms under cool water. In a 3 quart sauce pot, add the dried mushrooms to the hot stock or water and bring to a simmer. Reduce the stock to 6-7 cups. When reduced, strain stock through a sieve 2 or 3 times, and then through cheese cloth to remove mushroom particles. If using the stock immediately, keep on low heat. If not, cool and refrigerate until ready to use.

FOR THE RISOTTO:

In a 6 quart heavy bottom sauce pan, heat the olive oil and sauté the onions over medium heat until translucent, about 3-5 minutes. Add rice and stir with wooden spoon until the rice kernels are coated with the oil. Increase heat to medium high and add stock ½ cup at a time. It is important to keep stirring the rice mixture. It is equally important to keep the rice and stock at a simmer. Once the stock has been absorbed, add another ½ cup. At this point, when the stock has been absorbed, add the mushrooms with the next ½ cup stock. Continue the process ½ cup of stock at a time, stirring constantly and waiting until the stock has been absorbed before adding more stock. Continue the process until the rice is creamy and tender. This process will take at least 20-25 minutes. If the rice is still firm and the stock is gone, add several tablespoons of hot water, waiting until the rice has absorbed the liquid before adding more. Remove the pan from the stove and vigorously stir in the butter and arugula. When the butter is incorporated and the arugula is wilted, add the parmigiano and continue to stir. To taste, add salt and pepper. Serve immediately and pass additional parmigiano.

Joe Rillo

- 8 cups chicken stock or water
- ½ ounce dried porchini mushrooms or dried cèpes
- 1 tablespoon extra virgin olive oil
- 12 ounces onion, minced
- 1½ pound arborio rice
- 1 tablespoon butter
- ⅔ cup freshly grated Reggiano-Parmigiano
- salt and pepper to taste
- 1 bunch fresh arugula, washed and coarsely chopped
- 1 pound exotic or domestic mushrooms, sliced i.e. crimini, shiitake, portobello, oyster, etc.

*At far left, **An Example from a Series of Publications by the PP&L Cooking School** -CCHS*

Sauces and Accompaniments

Cranberry Sauce

Makes One Quart

Make this sauce at Thanksgiving and then enjoy it throughout the year.

- 12 ounces fresh cranberries
- 1½ cups water
- 1 tablespoon Sure-Jel
- 3 cups sugar

In a saucepan, bring water, Sure-Jel and cranberries to a boil until cranberries pop or break open. Put cranberry mixture through a foodmill to remove skins. Pour mixture into a 3 quart saucepan and add sugar. Bring to a full, rolling boil. Boil for 2 minutes. Pour into mold or seal in jelly glasses. May be kept in air-tight container in the refrigerator for one year.

Helena B. Pickering

Cumberland Creek Tartare Sauce

Makes One Cup

A recipe passed down from great grandmother Guise.

- ¾ cup mayonnaise
- 1 tablespoon chopped stuffed olives
- 2 tablespoons lemon juice
- 1 tablespoon chopped parsley
- 2 tablespoons grated onion
- 3 tablespoons chopped pickles
- 1 teaspoon paprika

Add all ingredients to the mayonnaise. Combine thoroughly. Chill. Serve with fish.

Sondra Wolfe Elias

Overleaf, **Shippensburg Fair**
Mrs. Eugene Hoch looks at prize winning entries
1968

-CCHS

CONEY ISLAND HOT DOG SAUCE

Makes Approximately One Quart

Create your own Hotchee dogs.

Brown meat. Grind fine. Add all ingredients and simmer for 20 minutes.

Arlene Wentzel

- ½ pound ground beef
- 12 ounce can tomato paste
- 3 cups water
- ½ cup pickle relish
- 2 tablespoons chopped onion
- 2 tablespoons prepared mustard
- 3 teaspoons chili powder
- 2 teaspoons salt
- 2 teaspoons sugar

SAUCE INDIENNE

Makes One Cup

Spices up vegetables with an Indian flair.

In a food processor, process ginger and garlic with water. Set aside. Heat oil over medium heat in frying pan. Throw in the fennel seeds. Five seconds later, add the garlic-ginger water. Keep stirring until the water is almost gone. Add all remaining ingredients and simmer gently for 20 minutes. Serve with steamed broccoli or cauliflower, fried zucchini or eggplant, hot or ice cold. Keeps very well.

Oliver Hazan

- 1 cubic inch fresh ginger
- 6 cloves garlic
- ¼ cup water
- 1 teaspoon whole fennel seeds
- 6 tomatoes, chopped
- 1 teaspoon ground cumin
- 1 tablespoon ground coriander
- ½ teaspoon turmeric
- 2 teaspoons salt and pepper to taste
- ¼ cup oil

Raisin Sauce for Ham

Serves Six

Three generations have enjoyed this recipe.

- ½ cup packed brown sugar
- ¼ teaspoon dry mustard
- 1¼ tablespoons cornstarch
- ¼ teaspoon salt
- ¼ teaspoon cinnamon
  sprinkle of cloves and allspice
- ¼ cup vinegar
- 1 cup water
- 1 cup raisins

Mix dry ingredients. Add vinegar, water and raisins. Cook and stir until sauce thickens and raisins are plump, approximately 15 minutes.

Nancy Wilson

Oyster Sauce for Ham

Serves Six

Apparently, this was Washington's favorite sauce for Martha's hams.

- 1 pint oysters with their liquor
- ⅛ teaspoon ground mace
- 1 cup dry white wine
- 3 tablespoons flour
- 3 tablespoons butter

Cook butter and flour to make roux. Place the oysters in a saucepan, along with their own liquor. Add the mace and bring to a simmer. When the oysters are plump, remove them from the pan. Add the wine to the juices and reduce. Add the roux to thicken. Return the oysters to the sauce and serve.

Carol Green

Hean Oyster Sauce

Serves Six

Tastes even better if made the day ahead.

Drain oysters, boil liquor and skim until clear. In another pan, sauté celery in butter until transparent. Stir in the oysters and skimmed liquor and milk. Thicken with flour paste. Add pepper. Cook 15 minutes slowly or the sauce will curdle. Serve decorated with first the sieved white and then the sieved yellow of the egg in center.

Elizabeth Hean Stone

- 1 pint (2 dozen) oysters (small)
- ½ cup chopped celery
- ½ cup milk
- 1-2 hard-boiled eggs - separated and sieved for topping
- 2 tablespoons butter
- ¼ teaspoon pepper
- 2 tablespoons flour plus ½ cup milk to thicken

To Pickle Oysters. An Old Recipe

Open one hundred of the finest and largest (rock) oysters you can get into a pan with all their liquor with them. Mind you do not cut them in opening as that will spoil their beauty. Wash them clean out of the liquor in a stew pan and give it a boil, then strain it through a sieve and let it stand half an hour to settle them. Pour it from the settings into a stew pan and put a half a pint of vinegar, a little salt, half an ounce of cloves and mace, a half pint of white wine, a little allspice, a whole pepper, a nutmeg cut in thin slices and a dozen of bay leaves. Boil it up five minutes then put in your oysters and give them a boil up for a minute or two.

Put them in your jars and when they are cold put a little sweet oil at the top and tye them down with a bladder and leather. Keep them in a cool, dry place and when you use them untie them, skim off the oil, put them in a dish with a little of the liquor and garnish with green parsley.

Peachy Parker's Cookbook

Spaghetti Sauce

Makes Six Quarts

Can be frozen up to six months without any loss of flavor or consistency.

- 8 tablespoons virgin olive oil
- 8 medium/large onions, chopped fine
- 2 green or red sweet bell peppers, chopped fine
- 5 ounces canned mushrooms, drained and chopped
- 9 large fresh or frozen tomatoes or equivalent, chopped
- 30 ounces (2-15 ounce cans) tomato sauce
- 18 ounces (3-6 ounce cans) tomato paste
- 2 teaspoons garlic powder (or equivalent chopped fresh cloves)
- 7 teaspoons salt (adjust to taste)
- 4 teaspoons oregano
- 4 teaspoons basil
- 4 teaspoons pepper
- 4 tablespoons sugar
- 2 teaspoons Italian seasoning

In a 6 quart dutch oven measure olive oil and add onion, garlic, chopped pepper and mushrooms. Cook stirring until vegetables are tender but not brown. Add tomato sauce, tomato paste and tomatoes. Add remaining ingredients and continue to simmer over low/medium heat 1½ to 2 hours (cannot be overcooked). Stir occasionally to prevent sticking. Thickness may be adjusted with liquid of your choice; water, wine, broth, etc.

Charles E. Maclay

Town Pump
*South Bedford Street near South Street
Carlisle
c. 1910
A. A. Line photographer*

-CCHS

BRANDIED PEACHES FOR HAM

Makes One Quart

A *nice accompaniment for any meat.*

Drain the peaches and reserve 1 cup of the juice. Mix the sugar with the reserved peach juice and boil until reduced to one half the original quantity. Cool, measure and stir in an equal amount of brandy, approximately ½ cup, and the almond extract. Pour brandy syrup over peaches and let sit at least 4 hours. Garnish ham with peaches.

Carol Green

2	13 ounce cans peach halves
1	cup granulated sugar
½	cup brandy, preferably a fruity brandy
3-4	drops almond extract

RHUBARB CHUTNEY

Makes One Quart

S *erve over warm brie.*

Bring sugar and vinegar to boil. Add remaining ingredients. Reduce heat and simmer for 20 to 30 minutes. Remove from heat. Cover and let stand until cool. Transfer chutney to a 1 quart container and chill. Keeps in the refrigerator for about 1 week.

Patty Armbrust

1	cup firmly packed light brown sugar
½	cup cider vinegar
3	cups chopped rhubarb
1	cup golden raisins
½	cup lemon, unpeeled, chopped
½	cup orange, unpeeled, chopped
2	teaspoons finely chopped ginger root
1	clove garlic, chopped
½	teaspoon each, cinnamon, salt and nutmeg
⅛	teaspoon cayenne pepper

SAUCES AND ACCOMPANIMENTS

Rhubarb Pineapple Compote

Serves Six to Eight

Simple, different and very good.

- 4 cups fresh diced rhubarb
- 1 cup sugar
- ½ teaspoon vanilla
- 2 cups fresh or canned drained pineapple chunks

Mix diced rhubarb with sugar in the top of a double boiler. Cook over boiling water about 40 minutes or until rhubarb is tender. Remove from heat, stir in vanilla and pineapple. Serve chilled.

June Slep

Homemade Mayonnaise

Makes Two Cups

There is an old wives tale that mayonnaise will not bind if made when a thunderstorm threatens or is in progress.

With portable mixer or wire whip, beat the egg yolks until pale and thickened. Add mustard, salt and vinegar. Beat for one minute. Then, by teaspoon driblets, begin beating in half of the oil. Then begin adding oil by tablespoon driblets beating after each addition. Never add too much oil for sauce to absorb. When sauce becomes too thick, add driblets of vinegar to thin out. Cover in small jar or bowl and refrigerate.

Ann Hays Jacobs

- 3 egg yolks
- 1/4 teaspoon dry mustard
- 1/2 teaspoon salt
- 2 teaspoons wine vinegar
- 2 cups fruity olive oil
- salt and pepper

Hot Mustard

Makes One Cup

Especially tasty as a spread for hot ham sandwiches.

Blend all ingredients well. Store in covered jar.

Mary Wheeler King

- 1/2 cup brown sugar
- 1/2 cup cider vinegar
- 3 ounces dry mustard

At left, **Shank and Bowman Canning Factory**
Corporation Street
Newville
1938

-Shippensburg Historical Society Collection

MANITOBA PICKLES

Makes Six Pints

These are great with ham or beef, or just on buttered biscuits or toast.

- 2 dozen pickling cucumbers, sliced thin
- 1 dozen pearl onions, peeled and sliced thin
- 1 cup Kosher salt
- 2 cups brown sugar
- ½ cup flour
- 1 tablespoon turmeric
- 1 tablespoon dry mustard
- ½ tablespoon curry
- 1 quart vinegar

Put sliced cucumbers and onions in large glazed glass or stainless steel bowl. Pour over 1 cup Kosher salt and cover with water. Seal with Saran Wrap and let stand in ice box over night. In the morning, drain pickles. Taste for saltiness and rinse lightly, if necessary. Prepare sauce: mix together dry ingredients carefully to avoid lumps. Add vinegar, bring to gentle boil, add cucumbers and onions. Bring to a boil again to scald cucumbers and onions. Pack in jars, seal and process in boiling water bath for 10 minutes.

Hermione Saegmuller

Note

Pickling takes time and patience. Have jars hot in dishwasher and put them in a pan of hot water to fill. Poke full jars with knife to force out air bubbles. Don't screw lids tight before processing. Wipe edges of jars before placing lid on. They won't seal if there's any food on the rim. Let cool on a rack after processing and listen for the "blips" as they seal.

Pickles - For 1000 Small, Whole Cucumbers

Take 1000 small, whole cucumbers and put them in a crock with layers of coarse salt: pour boiling water over them, cover closely with a coarse cloth and let them stand 24 hours, then wipe them dry.

To three gallons of good vinegar take 1/2 lb. of sliced horse-radish

- 4 crushed nutmegs
- 1 oz. of whole cloves
- 1 oz of allspice
- 2 lbs. light brown sugar
- 1 box ground mustard
- 1/2 lb. crushed green ginger
- 1/4 lb. celery seed

Mix together and put in the jar a layer of cucumbers and spices till all are in; then pour over the boiling vinegar: if you can get 50 small onions and 2 dozen cloves of garlic put in at the same time, but they can be added later: also, if you like, 1 oz. turmeric mixed with a little vinegar. Add to them a few small pieces of alum to equal the size of a walnut, which is necessary to make them crisp. 1 oz each of black and white mustard seed may be added and some green and red hot peppers.

When the pickle is perfectly cold, pour over the top one bottle of olive oil. This must be stirred through every time any pickles are taken out as it will always rise to the top.

Peachy Parker's Cookbook

Marvelous Marmalade

Makes Five Quarts

Friends always look forward to receiving a jar of this marmalade from Mrs. McCrea.

- 1 lemon
- 1 grapefruit
- 1 orange
- 12 cups sugar
- water

Juice fruit. Measure juice. Cut rind and add to juice to make one quart. Add an additional orange and/or lemon to make exactly one quart if necessary.

Day 1: Add 3 quarts water to 1 quart juice and rind. Let sit for 24 hours.

Day 2: Put liquid into a large pot and boil for 10 minutes. Let sit for 24 hours.

Day 3: Add sugar (5 pounds equals about 11 cups). Boil until it jells at least 2 to 3 hours and sometimes much longer. Test by putting a dab on a clean saucer. On a gloomy day, it takes longer. Put into clean jars and cover with paraffin when cool.

Harriet McCrea

Sunny Strawberry Preserves

Makes Three Quarts

Warm, sunny days produce the best preserves.

- 2 quarts strawberries
- 2 quarts sugar

Combine strawberries and sugar and let set overnight. Boil for 10 minutes and set in the sun for 2 to 3 days until thick. Seal with paraffin.

Pauline Raiser-Kee

Grape Jam

Makes One Quart

T*ry this on your next peanut butter sandwich.*

Boil grapes and sugar for 20 minutes. Run through a sieve and seal while hot.

Pauline Raiser-Kee

- **4 cups grapes**
- **3 cups sugar**

Lemon Butter

Makes Two Cups

T*his is a traditional Pennsylvania Quaker recipe. It is similar to Lemon Curd and wonderful on warm rolls or bread.*

In the top of a double boiler, beat eggs slightly and beat in sugar. Cook together, stirring occasionally. When eggs and sugar are cooked, add lemon juice and rind and cook slightly. (This will thicken a bit.) Add butter and remove from the stove. Blend well.

Virginia A. LaFond

- **6 eggs**
- **2 cups sugar**
- **juice of 3 lemons**
- **grated rind of one lemon**
- **¼ pound butter**

Accompaniments

Making Apple Butter
1907
-CCHS, *Postcard Collection*

Apple Butter

Makes Nine Quarts

This recipe was brought to Cumberland County by early German settlers. Boiling of apple butter over an open fire was a festive time in many farm homes. Neighbors, friends, and relatives would gather in a family kitchen the evening before the apples were to be cooked. The women peeled, cored and quartered the apples, while the men split the wood. Locust wood was preferred.

The making of apple butter required much wood, a copper kessel (kettle), and a long handled wooden paddle. It is an all day affair. The cider needs to boil uncovered until it is half its original quantity. The apples and sugar are then added and allowed to boil only a few minutes before the heat is reduced. The kettle is kept uncovered throughout the cooking to allow constant stirring with a long handled wooden paddle to avoid scorching. The spices are added after the apples become smeary and begin to thicken. Cook until thick enough to spread. Store the apple butter after cooling in crocks and seal with waxed cloth.

- 1 bushel of apples (McIntosh, Cortland, or Baldwin)
- 11 gallons of sweet apple cider
- 11 pounds of sugar
- 5½ tablespoons cinnamon
- 5½ tablespoons allspice or ginger
- 2½ tablespoons cloves

Wayne Rutz Family

Note

Apple butter was often eaten with Schmierkase (cottage cheese). The ladies took great pride in showing their apple butter at fairs and Granger's socials.

Breakfast

Broccoli Ham Rollups

Serves Eight

Delicious complement to your favorite egg dish.

- 1 head broccoli, cut into spears
- 8 slices cooked ham
- 8 slices Swiss cheese
- 2 large sweet onions
- 2 tablespoons flour
- ½ teaspoon thyme
- 2 cups milk
- Parmesan cheese

Preheat oven to 350°. Steam broccoli with pinch of oregano until al dente. Place slices of cheese on top of slice of ham. Top with a spear of broccoli and roll up. Place in a large casserole dish seam side down.

TO MAKE THE SAUCE

Slice onions into rings. Sauté lightly in butter. Add flour, thyme and milk. Stir until smooth and thick. Pour over rollups, sprinkle with Parmesan cheese and bake for 30 minutes or until heated through.

Mary Caverly

At right, **G. H. Bender Grocery Store**
24 South Pitt Street
Carlisle
c. 1910

-CCHS, Griffith Collection

Overleaf, **Odorless Egg Case Filler Mfg. Co.**
Shippensburg
1898
D. C. Moll photographer

-Shippensburg Historical Society Collection

BRUNCH BAKE

Serves Eight to Ten

A medley of fresh fruit and toasted English muffins with homemade jam make a delicious, easily prepared Sunday Brunch.

Cube bread, add melted butter or margarine and mix well. In buttered 13 X 9 inch pan, layer ingredients as follows: Half of the bread cubes, half of the cheese, half of the vegetables, all of the ham, then remaining vegetables, cheese and bread cubes. Beat eggs and milk thoroughly with seasonings. Pour over all layers. Refrigerate overnight or at least 2 hours. Bake in a preheated oven at 350° for one hour or until puffy and lightly browned. Let sit 5 to 10 minutes following baking before cutting.

Judy Castrina

- 8 slices white bread
- 3/4 cup melted butter or margarine
- 2 cups cubed cooked ham (smoked is more flavorful)
- 10 ounces chopped cooked broccoli
- 10 ounces chopped cooked spinach
- 2 cups shredded sharp Cheddar cheese
- 4 eggs
- 2 cups milk
- 1 teaspoon salt
- 1/2 teaspoon pepper

Scrambled Eggs Pie

Serves Six

Appetizing holiday breakfast or brunch casserole that can be made the night before.

- 1 cup coarsely crushed corn flakes cereal
- 2 tablespoons margarine or butter, melted
- ¼ cup margarine or butter
- 8 eggs
- ½ cup milk
- 1 tablespoon snipped chives
- ½ teaspoon seasoned salt
- ⅛ teaspoon pepper
- 6 slices bacon, crisply fried and crumbled
- 3 slices American cheese, cut diagonally into halves

Preheat oven to 375°. Mix cereal with 2 tablespoons melted margarine or butter; reserve ¼ cup cereal mixture. Spread remaining cereal mixture in ungreased 9 inch pie plate or quiche dish. Heat ¼ cup margarine or butter in 10 inch skillet over medium heat until melted. Beat eggs, milk, chives, seasoned salt and pepper with a hand beater. Pour egg mixture into skillet; add bacon. Cook over low heat stirring gently, just until eggs are almost set. Quickly spoon into pie plate. Arrange cheese, overlapping slightly, around edge of plate. Sprinkle with reserved cereal mixture. This dish can be covered and refrigerated at this point for no longer than 24 hours. To serve immediately, heat uncovered in oven for 10-15 minutes or until cheese melts and eggs are firm. To serve after refrigeration, heat in 375° oven 25-30 minutes.

Eve Wilkie

Egg Omelet For Twelve

Serves Twelve

Serve with grilled tomato halves, fruit, and fresh bread for an easy and hearty breakfast.

Preheat oven to 325°. Melt butter in bottom of a large glass pan (at least 13x9x2 inches). Mix ingredients and pour into pan. Bake until set, 40 to 45 minutes.

Margaret Bushey

¼	cup butter
1½	dozen large eggs
1	cup sour cream
1	cup milk
2	teaspoons salt
½	cup chopped onion
1	large jar marinated artichoke hearts, chopped
3-4	cups chopped mushrooms, mixture of shiitaki, crimini, porcini
1	cup mozzarella cheese, grated

Egg Souffle

Serves Eight to Ten

Sunday brunch menu: Egg Souffle and Broccoli Ham Rollups.

Preheat oven to 400°. Put saltines in a buttered 8x12 inch casserole or souffle dish. Combine remaining ingredients and pour over saltines. Bake for 45 minutes.

Patti Owen

28-30	saltine crackers, crumbled
2	cups sharp cheddar cheese, grated
6	eggs, beaten
½	cup margarine, melted
	salt and pepper to taste
3	cups milk (may use skim)

Breakfast

Fritatta

Serves Six to Eight

An egg dish that adapts to almost anything in your cupboard.

- 6 large eggs at room temperature
  salt and freshly ground pepper, to taste
  freshly grated nutmeg, to taste
- 4 cups loosely packed fresh spinach leaves, rinsed, dried and finely chopped
- 1 cup freshly grated Parmesan or Romano cheese
- 1 tablespoon extra-virgin olive oil

Preheat the oven broiler. Crack the eggs into a large bowl and beat lightly with a fork. Add the salt and pepper, nutmeg, spinach and half the cheese, and beat lightly to combine the ingredients. In a 9-inch ovenproof omelet pan or skillet, heat the oil over moderate heat, swirling the pan to coat the bottom and sides evenly. When the oil is hot but not smoking, add the frittata mixture. Reduce the heat to low and cook slowly, stirring the top two-thirds of the mixture (leaving the bottom part to set, so it doesn't stick) until the eggs have formed small curds and the frittata is brown on the bottom and almost firm in the center, about 4 minutes. The top should still be very soft. With a spatula, lightly loosen the frittata from the edges of the pan, to prevent sticking later on. Sprinkle with the remaining cheese. Transfer the pan to the broiler, placing it about 5 inches from the heat, so that the frittata cooks without burning. Broil until the frittata browns lightly on top and becomes puffy and firm, about 2 minutes. (Watch carefully: A minute can make the difference between a golden-brown frittata and one that's overcooked.) Remove the frittata from the broiler and let cool in the pan for 2 minutes. Place a large flat plate over the top of the pan and invert the frittata onto it. Let the frittata cool to room temperature. To serve, cut into wedges and serve at brunch or with a salad or as a sandwich filling. Can substitute chopped baked ham, sliced mushrooms, chopped green onions, Swiss or Cheddar instead of spinach and Parmesan or Romano cheese.

Licia Sandberg

Versatile Cheese Strata

Serves Six to Eight

Options are endless: substitute shrimp, ham, bacon, sausage, chicken or turkey for the crab.

Cut crusts from bread. Place six slices in buttered 2-quart shallow casserole. Mix together remaining ingredients. Pour half of egg mixture over bread. Layer with remaining bread and egg mixture. Cover and refrigerate overnight. Preheat oven to 350°. Bake covered for 45 minutes. Remove cover and bake 30 minutes more. Serve immediately.

Mabel Torrence

12	slices white bread
½	pound Cheddar cheese, shredded
½	stick butter, melted
6	eggs, beaten
2	cups milk
1	teaspoon parsley flakes
½	cup thinly sliced mushrooms
1	6 ounce can crabmeat

To Make Good Boiled Coffee

2 heaping tablespoonsful of finely ground mocha and java to each person and one to the coffee pot.

Add one egg and shell and enough cold water to thoroughly moisten the coffee grounds.

Add to this freshly boiled and boiling water, one kitchen cupful to each tablespoonful of coffee. As soon as it begins to boil, time it and boil twenty-five minutes exactly. Put in a dash of cold water, set for a moment to the side of the range and then pour off.

In pouring off boiled coffee it is always advisable to strain through a piece of cheesecloth laid in a fine strainer.

Peachy Parker's Cookbook

Popover Pie

Serves Four

Eggs-"traordinary". Don't forget the raspberry sauce.

- 3 eggs
- 3/4 cup flour
- 3/4 cup milk
- 2-3 tablespoons butter

Preheat oven to 425°. Place butter into glass pie pan and put in oven to melt. Mix eggs, flour and milk gently. Remove pan from oven and pour in ingredients. Bake for 20 minutes.

Paula Price

Raspberry Sauce

Makes One Cup

Perfect accompaniment to Popover Pie or over Peach ice cream.

- 2 12 ounce bags frozen raspberries
- 2 teaspoons freshly squeezed lemon juice
- 2/3 cup sugar

Thaw raspberries in strainer placed over a bowl. This can take several hours. There should be about 1 cup of juice. In a saucepan, boil the juice until reduced to 1/4 cup. Pour into lightly oiled glass bowl. (The juice can be reduced in the microwave on high power. Use at least a 4 cup glass bowl so that it will not boil over.) Puree the raspberries, remove the seeds with a fine disk food mill or force them through a fine strainer. There will be one cup of puree. Stir in the syrup, lemon juice and sugar. Stir well. This can be frozen and used as needed.

Paula Price

Pear and Apple Compote

Serves Six

This is wonderful with almost any brunch—a delicious way to enjoy the best of winter fruit.

Bring juice, wine, honey, cinnamon and nutmeg to a boil and simmer 10 minutes. Add apples and zests. Simmer 3 minutes. Add pears and simmer 3 minutes more. Add raisins to hot mixture. Cool. Refrigerate overnight. Serve in bowls with small dollop of whipped cream sprinkled with cinnamon.

Margaret Bushey

2¼	cups unsweetened, unfiltered apple juice
1	cup dry white wine
2	tablespoons honey
1	3 inch cinnamon stick
¼	teaspoon nutmeg
3	medium apples, cored, pared, sliced
	zest of 1 lemon julienne
	zest of 1 orange julienne
3	pears, cored, pared, sliced
½	cup golden raisins, currants, or combination
	whipped cream for garnish

Ad from the Carlisle Directory
1924
-CCHS

Breakfast Squares

Serves Eight to Ten

For a special breakfast, serve with fresh fruit and sticky buns.

- 6 eggs
- 1 cup milk
- 2 teaspoons sugar
- 1 teaspoon salt
- ½ cup flour
- 1 teaspoon baking powder
- ½ pound Cheddar cheese, shredded
- 3 ounces cream cheese, cubed
- 8 ounces cottage cheese
- ¾ stick butter, cubed
- ½ pound sausage, bacon or ham, cooked

Preheat oven to 350°. In small bowl, beat eggs, milk, sugar and salt. In larger bowl, stir together flour and baking powder. Add liquid ingredients, beating well. Mix in cheese and butter. Pour into greased 11"x13" pan. Sprinkle with meat. Bake for 40 minutes.

Paula Price

Pennsylvania Fresh Corn Fritters

Makes Twelve Small Fritters

Classic corn fritters.

- 2 eggs, separated
- 2 cups fresh corn kernels
- 2 tablespoons sugar
- ½ teaspoon salt
- 1 slice bread, crumbled

Mix together egg yolks, corn, sugar, salt and bread crumbs. Beat egg whites until stiff. Fold corn mixture into egg whites. Drop from spoon on to buttered hot griddle or skillet. Fry, one side at a time, until golden brown. Serve immediately.

Tita Eberly

Aunt Christine's Breakfast Cake

Serves Six to Eight

Stirs up memories of kitchens past.

Preheat oven to 350°. Mix butter, baking powder, sugar and flour to a cornmeal consistency saving one-half of the mixture for the topping. Add to one-half of the mixture, the eggs, milk and vanilla. Continue beating until thoroughly mixed. Put this mixture into a 8 or 9 inch greased pan. Sprinkle with remaining topping. Bake for 30 minutes.

Karen Diener Best

- ¼ pound butter
- 2 teaspoons baking powder
- 2 cups sugar
- 3 cups flour
- 3 eggs
- 1 cup milk
- 1 teaspoon vanilla

Crumb Pies

Serves Eight to Twelve

This is delicious when eaten slightly warm with a good cup of coffee and a friend. These crumb pies were originally made in "dough trays".

Preheat oven to 350°. Mix the flour, sugar, shortening, nutmeg and cinnamon in a large bowl. Take out enough to use for crumbs on top (be generous). Add 1 egg and mix. In a small bowl mix together soda and cream of tartar into the buttermilk. Add this mixture into the flour mixture. Blend well. Pour into 2 medium sized lightly greased pie pans. Add crumbs. Bake for 40 to 45 minutes.

Maurita B. Diller

- 2½ cups all purpose flour
- 1 cup white sugar
- ½ cup butter or margarine (soft)
- 1 teaspoon nutmeg
- 1 teaspoon cinnamon
- 1 egg
- 1 cup buttermilk
- ½ teaspoon soda
- ⅛ teaspoon cream of tartar

Breakfast

Cream Scones

Makes Six to Eight Three Inch Scones

These were served at the first Celtic Festival at the Two Mile House.

- 2 cups flour
- 4 tablespoons butter
- 4 teaspoons baking powder
- 2 eggs
- 2 teaspoons sugar
- ½ cup cream or milk
- ½ teaspoon salt

Preheat oven to 450°. Mix and sift dry ingredients. Work in butter with pastry mixer, fork or fingertips. Add well beaten eggs (reserving small amount of white for glaze) and cream. Toss on floured board, pat and roll ¾" thick. Cut in squares, diamonds or triangles. Brush with reserved egg white, diluted with 1 teaspoon water. Sprinkle with sugar and bake for 15 minutes.

Sara Shoemaker

Sour Cream Coffeecake

Serves Ten to Twelve

A sweet way to start the day.

- 2 sticks sweet butter
- 2¾ cups granulated sugar
- 3 eggs, beaten
- 2 cups all purpose flour
- 1 tablespoon baking powder
- ½ teaspoon salt
- 2 cups sour cream
- 1 tablespoon vanilla
- 2 cups chopped pecans
- 1 tablespoon cinnamon

Preheat oven to 350°. Grease and flour a 10 inch bundt pan. Cream together butter and 2 cups sugar. Add well beaten eggs. Add sour cream and vanilla. Sift together flour, baking powder and salt. Fold dry ingredients into the creamed mixture. Beat until just blended. Do not overbeat. In a separate bowl, mix remaining ¾ cup sugar, pecans and cinnamon. Put ½ of the pecan mixture in the bottom of the pan. Pour ½ of the batter on top of the pecan mixture. Sprinkle with the rest of the pecan mixture. Add remaining batter. Bake on the middle rack of the oven for 60 minutes or until a cake tester comes out clean. May be served warm.

Mary Katherine Dennin

Sticky Buns

Serves Eight to Ten

What could be better than these sticky buns, a cup of coffee and the Sunday paper?

In a large bowl, dissolve yeast in warm water. Set aside. In a saucepan, heat milk until bubbles appear around edge or a skin forms. Cool milk to lukewarm by adding shortening, ¼ cup sugar and salt. To the yeast, add half of the flour, the milk mixture and the beaten egg. Mix with spoon until smooth. Add enough remaining flour to handle easily. Turn dough onto lightly floured surface and knead until smooth, about 5 minutes. "Plop" dough into a well-greased large bowl and turn over. Cover with a damp, smooth towel or plastic wrap sprayed with cooking-oil spray. Let rise in a warm place until doubled in size. (About 1½ hours.) Punch down and let rise again. Roll out to a rectangle (about 10" x 18"), spread with 2 tablespoons softened butter and leave the edge of one of the 18" sides free of butter. Sprinkle with ½ cup sugar and 2 teaspoons cinnamon. Roll up tightly, starting with the 18" side opposite the unbuttered edge, and seal by pinching unbuttered edge to the roll. Cut into 1" slices and place in pan which has been prepared with sticky mixture (below). Let rise until double. Bake in a preheated 375° oven for 25-30 minutes or until brown and rolls sound hollow when tapped. Immediately turn onto large tray and let sticky mixture drain briefly, then lift pan off.

TO MAKE THE STICKY MIXTURE

In a saucepan, melt butter, brown sugar and corn syrup together until mixture comes just to a boil. Pour into sprayed 9"x13" pan and sprinkle with raisins and/or nuts.

Jane Lerch

- ¼ cup warm water
- 1 package active dry yeast
- 3½ to 3¾ cups flour
- ¾ cup milk
- ¼ cup sugar
- 1 teaspoon salt
- 1 egg, beaten
- ¼ cup shortening, room temperature
- 2 tablespoons softened butter
- ½ cup sugar
- 2 teaspoons cinnamon

For Sticky Mixture
- ½ cup butter
- ¾ cup packed brown sugar
- 1½ tablespoons light corn syrup

250th Anniversary of George Washington's Visit to Carlisle
*L to R, Hubert Gilroy, William Sommerfield (George Washington) , Wayne Powell, Skip Ebert,
Linda Witmer, Executive Director CCHS, a Sentinel photographer, Leroy Mooney and Philip Hunter
West Pennsboro Township
1994*

-CCHS, Gift of Carol Green

Cinnamon Twists

Makes Two Dozen

This recipe is long but easy and very rewarding. Family and friends will devour every one.

Dissolve yeast in water. Stir other ingredients together. Turn dough onto a floured board and fold several times to smooth. Roll dough into a 24 x 6 inch oblong. Spread with additional 2 tablespoons soft butter. Sprinkle half of the length of dough with the filling. Fold the other half over. Cut into 24, 1 inch wide strips. Hold both ends of each strip and twist in opposite directions. Place on greased baking sheets 2 inches apart. Press both ends of each strip to baking sheet. Cover with a towel and let rise until doubled, about 1 hour. Bake in a preheated 375° oven 12 to 15 minutes until golden brown. Frost with icing while warm.

Margaret Bushey

For the Twists
- ¼ cup warm water
- 1 tablespoon active dry yeast
- ¾ cup lukewarm sour cream
- 3 tablespoons sugar
- ⅛ teaspoon soda
- 1 teaspoon salt
- 1 large egg
- 2 tablespoons soft butter
- 3 cups flour

For the Filling
- 2 tablespoons butter
- ⅓ cup brown sugar
- 1 teaspoon cinnamon

For the Icing
- 1½ cups confectioners sugar
- 1 teaspoon vanilla
- milk or cream to moisten

George Washington Hunt Breakfast Menu

Stirrup Cup
Spirits and Juices

Hunter's Stew
Bucksnort Ham with Brandied Peaches
Smoked Turkey

English Garden Salad
King's Arms Sweet Potatoes
Pickled Red Cabbage
Glazed Autumn Vegetables
Ambrosia

Spoon Bread

Whiskey Cake St. Hubert
Cheese Pie
Bourbon Balls

UNCLE ANNIE'S FAMOUS PANCAKES

Serves Four

Not your ordinary pancakes!

- 4 eggs, beaten
- 1 cup buttermilk
- ½ cup cottage cheese
- ¼ cup sour cream
- 1 cup Bisquick
- ½ cup beer

Beat eggs, add buttermilk, cottage cheese, sour cream and Bisquick. Let stand 10 minutes. Preheat griddle until very hot. Just before spooning onto griddle, add ½ cup beer. Do not omit. Better if made silver dollar size.

Andrea Sheya

WHOLE WHEAT PANCAKES

Serves Six

These call for real maple syrup.

- 2 eggs
- 2 cups buttermilk
- 3 tablespoons vegetable oil
- 1 teaspoon baking soda
- ½ teaspoon salt
- 1½ teaspoons baking powder
- 1 teaspoon sugar
- 1 cup whole wheat flour
- 1 cup white flour

Beat together eggs, buttermilk and vegetable oil. Add dry ingredients and mix until blended together. More buttermilk or regular milk may be added to get desired consistency. Cook pancakes on a preheated hot greased griddle or frying pan on the top of the stove.

Carol Reed

Waffles

Makes Fourteen to Sixteen Four Inch Waffles

Good for breakfast or with chicken and gravy.

Beat egg whites until stiff; combine yolks, shortening and milk. Sift and add flour, salt, sugar and baking powder. Fold in egg whites. Prepare according to waffle iron instructions.

Ladies Auxiliary of North Middleton Township Fire Company

2	eggs, separated
¼	cup melted shortening
1⅔	cups milk
2	cups flour
1	tablespoon sugar
½	teaspoon salt
1	tablespoon baking powder

Receipt
1879

-CCHS, Gift of Nancy Wilson

Breakfast 215

Breads

Anise Bread

Makes Two Dozen

Similar to Italian biscotti.

- 4 eggs
- 1 pound powdered sugar
- 1 pound flour
- 1 tablespoon anise seed
- 1/4 teaspoon hartshorn (baking powder)

Stir eggs and sugar until light and fluffy. Add flour and beat with electric beater for ½ hour. Preheat oven to 325°. Sprinkle seeds on greased cookie sheet. Seeds may also be put in dough, or add ½ teaspoon anise seed oil. Spread dough ½ inch thick on baking sheet. Bake for about 30 minutes. When cold, cut in finger length pieces and toast under broiler.

Florence Jay

Carlisle Indian and Industrial School
Bakery
c. 1905
A. A. Line photographer

-CCHS

Overleaf, **H. C. Fry and Brothers Bakery**
North Earl Street
Shippensburg
c. 1913

-Shippensburg Historical Society Collection

Beer Bread

Makes One Loaf

Wonderful texture and taste, and easy too.

Preheat oven to 375°. Measure flour into bowl (don't shake down). Add sugar and mix. Add all of the beer at once and break egg over beer. Mix together but don't beat. Pour into a greased 9x5 bread pan. Bake on middle shelf of oven for 65 to 70 minutes.

Mary Jane Cooper

3½	cups self-rising flour
¼	cup granulated sugar
1	12 ounce can beer at room temperature
1	egg at room temperature

Dill Bread

Makes One Loaf

This recipe was submitted by a member of the Barnitz family, which operated a cornmeal and flour mill for four generations (1836-1947) on the Pine Road.

- 1 package dry yeast
- ¼ cup warm water
- 8 ounces cottage cheese
- ¼ cup melted butter
- 2 tablespoons sugar
- 1 tablespoon minced onion
- 1 tablespoon dill seed
- 1 tablespoon dill weed
- 1 teaspoon salt
- ¼ teaspoon baking soda
- 1 egg, well beaten
- 2½ cups flour

Soften yeast in water. Bring cottage cheese to room temperature. Stir in butter, sugar, onion, dill, salt and baking soda. Add yeast and beat in egg. Add flour to make a soft dough, knead for 5 minutes. Put in a greased bowl, cover, set to rise in a warm place for 1½ hours. Punch down, cover, and let rise ½ hour. Shape into loaf and put in greased loaf pan. Cover and let rise until double (about 45 minutes). Preheat oven to 350°. Bake for 15-20 minutes.

Barbara Barnitz Lillich

Hot Cheddar Cheese Bread

Serves Twelve

Delicious for lunch or supper with soup or salad.

- 1 pound loaf french bread, cut in half lengthwise
- 4 ounces (1 cup) shredded cheddar cheese
- ¼ cup mayonnaise
- 3 tablespoons chopped green onions
- ½ teaspoon chili powder
- 2 tablespoons sliced black olives, optional

Preheat oven to 350°. In a small bowl, combine cheese, mayonnaise and chili powder; stir until well mixed. Spread each half of bread with cheese mixture to within ½ inch of edge. Arrange olive slices over cheese. Wrap each bread half in foil. Bake for 10 to 15 minutes or until thoroughly heated and cheese is melted.

Marilyn Aust

At right, "Grand Muller" Alice Moore
Two Mile House
South Middleton Township
c. 1925

-CCHS, Moore Collection

Onion Cheese Bread

Serves Six to Eight

Quick and easy.

Preheat oven to 400°. Cook onion in small amount of oil until tender but not brown. Combine egg and milk. Add to biscuit mix until mix is just moistened. Add onion and half of the cheese and parsley. Spread dough in greased 8" round cake pan. Sprinkle with remaining cheese. Drizzle melted butter over the top. Bake for 20 minutes or until toothpick comes out clean.

Joan F. Bobb

½ cup chopped onion
1 egg, beaten
½ cup milk
1½ cups "Bisquick" or any biscuit mix
1 cup shredded sharp cheese
2 tablespoons snipped parsley
2 tablespoons melted butter

BREADS

FOCACCIA

Serves Eight

Well *worth the effort.*

Cover potato with cold water in medium saucepan. Simmer until potato is tender, drain, reserve cooking liquid. Mash or rice the potato and measure out 1 cup. Meanwhile, sprinkle yeast over ½ cup warm water in a small bowl, stir to dissolve. Let stand 5 minutes and then mix in 3 tablespoons of flour. Cover bowl with plastic wrap and let stand in a warm, draft free area for ½ hour. Blanch rosemary and garlic in a small sauce pan for one minute. Strain, and add enough water to potato liquid to make 2 cups. Mix in rosemary, garlic and 2 tablespoons of olive oil. Combine 6½ cups flour and 1 tablespoon salt in a large bowl. Stir down yeast mixture and add to flour with herb-water mixture and 1 cup mashed or riced potato. Mix until sticky dough forms. Knead on well-floured surface until dough is smooth and elastic, about 10 minutes. Add more flour if sticky. Oil a large bowl, add dough, turning to coat entire surface. Cover bowl with plastic wrap and let rise in a warm, draft free spot for about 1 to 1½ hours. Punch dough down, knead on lightly floured surface until smooth, about 2 to 3 minutes, cover and let rest about 10 minutes. Grease a rimmed 9x13" jelly roll pan, roll out dough on lightly floured surface to 9x13" rectangle, transfer to prepared pan. Brush top with 2 tablespoons oil, sprinkle lightly with coarse salt and generously with pepper. Let rise in a warm, draft free area until almost double, about 1¼ hours. Bake in preheated 400° oven until bread is brown and sounds hollow when tapped, about 40 minutes. Cool in pan for about 10 minutes and then transfer to rack. Put small amount of extra virgin olive oil on small plate with freshly ground pepper. Dip bread pieces in oil instead of using butter.

Judy Gallo Black

- 1 10 ounce boiling potato, peeled
- 1 tablespoon dry yeast (2 packages)
- ½ cup warm water, 105° to 115°
- 3 tablespoons bread flour
- 2 tablespoons minced, fresh rosemary
- 2 tablespoons minced garlic
- 2 tablespoons extra virgin olive oil
- 7 cups bread flour
- 1 tablespoon salt
- 2 tablespoons olive oil
  coarse Kosher salt
  fresh ground pepper

At left, **Old Draw-well**
*East South Street
Carlisle
c. 1905
Colonel Thomas Sharp photographer*

-CCHS

BREADS

FRENCH BREAD

Makes Two to Three Loaves

*G*ood recipe for beginning bread makers.

For the Batter
- 1 tablespoon dried yeast or 1 yeast cake
- 1 cup lukewarm water
- ½ teaspoon sugar
- 1½ cups flour, more or less

For the Bread
- 1 tablespoon salt
- ½ cup water
- 1 tablespoon yeast
- 1 cup lukewarm water
- 2 tablespoons dried non-fat milk
- 4 cups flour, more or less
- ½ teaspoon oil or butter

TO MAKE THE BATTER

Three days before baking, dissolve yeast in water, add sugar to proof. Add enough flour to make runny batter. Cover with plastic wrap and put in a cool, dark area. Uncover and stir each day.

TO MAKE THE BREAD

On baking day, dissolve yeast in 4 ounces water and add to 3 day old batter. Dissolve yeast in another cup of lukewarm water and proof, about five minutes. Add the batter. Stir in dried non-fat milk. Add flour, one cup at a time until you have a shaggy mass of dough. A wooden spoon works best for this process. Scrape down the bowl and dump the mose of dough onto a floured surface. Knead as long as you want to. It's good for the soul. At least knead the mose until it is smooth. It helps the flour to absorb the moisture by throwing the dough onto the counter surface 3 or 4 times. When you have a smooth dough and when it doesn't stick to a clean finger when you push on it, the dough is ready to rise. Put oil or butter in a large bowl and coat all of the inside of bowl. Place the dough in bowl and cover with plastic wrap and let rise in a cool place (65-70 degrees) for about two hours, or until it reaches the plastic wrap. When risen, dump the dough on a lightly floured surface and with a knife cut it into 3 or 4 elongated shapes. It is easiest to just squeeze the loaves into shape. Place on cookie sheets, 2 loaves per sheet, or in baguette tins that have been well dusted with corn meal. Make three slashes on top of each loaf with a very sharp knife, razor blade or kitchen scissors. This is necessary, because the yeast cells will expand with the next rise. Cover with a cloth, and once again let rise until double in size. After about one hour, preheat the oven to 450°. Set the rack in the lower third of the oven. If you use baking tiles, place them on the lowest rack. Spritz the bread with a water mister, when you place it in the oven. Spritz again after 5 minutes. Bake about 25 minutes or until the bread is golden brown in color. Remove from oven and place on a rack, so the bread does not sweat. Serve immediately.

George Kenneth Bishop

Note
Bread can be wrapped in foil and frozen. Uneaten bread will not mold if it is kept in the refrigerator well wrapped. If a piece goes dry, run water over it and place in moderate oven for 5 minutes. That will reconstitute the bread.

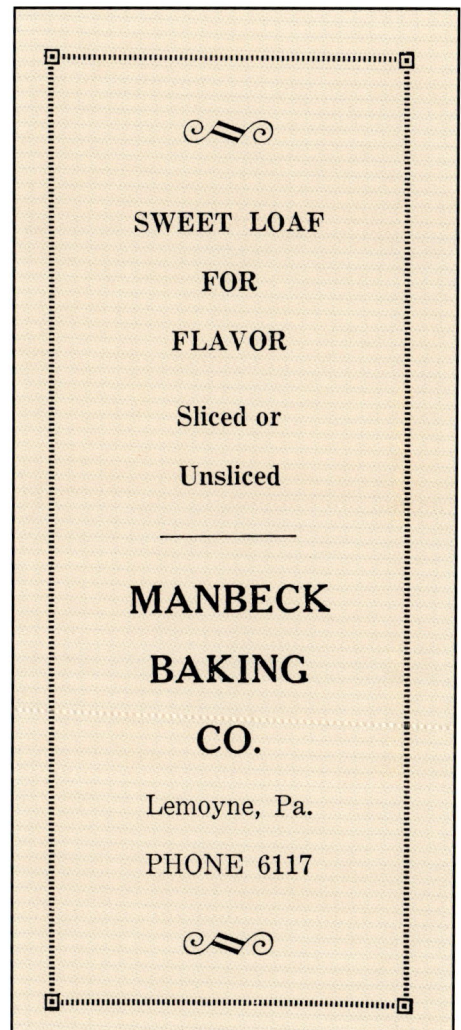

Ad from West Shore Directory
1932

-CCHS

Family Rolls

Makes Two Dozen Rolls

Two very good recipes in one, plain or sweet.

- 2 envelopes dry yeast
- ¼ cup lukewarm water
- 1 cup warm milk, not over 105°
- 1 teaspoon salt
- ½ stick of margarine
- ½ cup sugar
- 2 beaten eggs
- 5-6 cups flour

Dissolve yeast in water. Warm milk, add to margarine, sugar and salt. Stir and then add the beaten eggs. Check temperature. If not over 105°, add dissolved yeast. Stir in flour to make dough that can be lightly kneaded. Knead 10 minutes, let dough rest 10 minutes. Place in greased bowl. Turn dough over so that top is greased. Cover with plastic wrap and place in a cool oven. Put hot water in a large bowl and place in oven on a rack above the rising dough. Remove dough from oven once it has doubled in size. Roll out to ⅜ inch thick. Shape into parker house rolls or butter, add light brown sugar, cinnamon and roll up. Cut into 1" sections. Bake in greased pan at 325° for 15-20 minutes.

Janet Surick

French Rolls

Makes Twenty-four Rolls

Famous rolls from our own "California Cafe".

Reserve 1 cup flour. Mix all remaining ingredients in bowl until manageable. Turn onto floured surface and knead for 10 minutes, slowly incorporating reserved flour. Let rise for an hour in greased bowl in warm room. Punch down. Let rise again for an hour (or over night up to 72 hours, refrigerated and covered). Punch down. Dust two large cookie sheets with cornmeal. Cut dough into 24 chunks. Shape into balls between a flat hand and cupped hand. Place on sheets. Let rise for 45 minutes or longer if previously refrigerated. Preheat oven to 440°. Slice the top of the rolls with a sharp knife, quite deeply. With a water sprayer, lightly mist the rolls and generously spray the inside of the oven. Bake for 15 minutes. Rotate trays, top to bottom, front to back and left to right. Bake for at least 15 minutes more or until well colored. Use within 12 hours or freeze and re-heat in oven.

Oliver Hazan

- 7 cups all-purpose flour (optional, substitute 1/2 cup rye flour)
- 2 packages or tablespoons dry yeast
- 3 cups warm water (optional, substitute 1/2 cup buttermilk)
- 1 tablespoon salt

At left, **Baker, Charles Diller and his wife Annie**
George Weitzel on right, J. L. Farner on left
East Louther Street
Carlisle
c. 1905

-CCHS, Gift of Mildred Coller

Healthy Muffins

Makes Two Dozen Muffins

Start your day with these muffins or have them for a healthy and filling snack.

1½ cups whole wheat flour
½ cup oatmeal
1½ cups oat bran
1½ teaspoons cinnamon
½ teaspoon salt
1¼ teaspoons baking soda
1 teaspoon baking powder
1 tablespoon grated orange rind
1 cup grated apple
½ cup Brer Rabbit light molasses
2 beaten eggs or egg beater equivalent
2 tablespoons oil
½ cup raisins
juice of one orange
2 cups buttermilk

Preheat oven to 350°. Toss dry ingredients, or sift together. Stir in orange rind, apples, raisins. Combine orange juice, buttermilk, beaten eggs, molasses and oil. Stir liquid ingredients into dry. Pour into greased muffin tins (⅔ full) or cupcake papers in tins. Bake for 25 to 30 minutes.

Ginny Fickel Ehr

Front Menu Cover
New Way Restaurant (John Alexis)
1930
-CCHS

Honey Wheat Bread

Makes Two Large Loaves or Four Small Loaves

A *good wholesome bread.*

Combine margarine or butter, honey, water and cottage cheese in flat bottomed saucepan and place over medium heat. Remove from heat once it reaches 105° to 115°. In a large mixing bowl, place yeast, sugar, salt, egg, whole wheat flour and 1 cup of white flour. Add hot ingredients to flour mixture and beat at medium speed for 2 minutes. Gradually add remaining 4 cups of white flour while kneading with a bread hook. More white flour may be added to soft sticky dough so it is manageable. Place in greased bowl. Cover bowl with cloth and let rise until doubled, about 1 hour. Punch down dough, cut in half for two large loaves (or fourths for 4 small loaves) with a greased knife. Shape loaves on a floured surface. Place large loaves in two 9x5" greased tins or four 4x7 greased tins for small loaves. Cover with cloth and let rise about 1 hour or less. Bake in preheated 350° oven for 45 minutes to one hour or until medium dark brown. Bake 35 to 45 minutes for small loaves. Cool on wire rack. Remove pan when hot so crust will become hard. Best eaten warm. Great toasted the next few days.

Maureen Reed

⅓	cup margarine or butter
½	cup honey
1½	cups water
1	cup cottage cheese
2	packages yeast
2	tablespoons sugar
2	or less teaspoons salt
1	egg
1½	cups whole wheat flour
5	cups white bread flour

Cure for the Toothache

Alum, reduced to an impalpable powder, two drachms; nitrous spirits of ether, seven drachms. Mix and apply them to the tooth.

Peachy Parker's Cookbook

Breads

Pizza Dough

Makes Two Pizza Crusts

Rosario Maria Imbino Gallo's rolls may be made from this dough. Form dough into roll shapes, bake at 400° for 20 minutes or until rolls sound hollow when tapped on the bottom.

- 1 cup skim milk
- 1 cup water
- 2 tablespoons dry yeast
- 1 tablespoon sugar
- 1 tablespoon salt
- 5¼ cups bread flour
- 3 tablespoons olive oil

Heat milk and water to 105° to 115°. In a bowl dissolve yeast in liquid. Add sugar and salt. Stir and let stand for 5 minutes. Add 3 cups of the flour and the oil to liquid. Beat. Add remaining flour. Mix well. Place mixture on slightly floured board, forming a ball. Let stand 10 minutes. Knead for 10 minutes. Place in greased bowl. Cover. Let rise for 2 hours in a warm, draft-free place. Punch down. Dough can be refrigerated or frozen at this point. Divide dough in half. Place each piece of dough on a greased pizza pan. Stretch dough to shape of pan. Let dough rise again in warm area (about ½ hour). Preheat oven to 450°. Brush with additional oil on top of dough. Add sauce and desired toppings. Bake pizza for 2 minutes, then cover with aluminium pan (edges fitting pizza). Continue baking for 7 minutes. Remove cover. Continue to bake until bottom of crust is brown and cheese is melted. Remove pizza and place on wire rack.

Judy Gallo Black

Note

The type of pan is very important when making pizza. A heavy pizza pan or a heavy jelly roll pan will work, a cookie sheet must not be used.

At right, **Mrs. Melvin Long**
Home Baked Goods
Carlisle Farmers Market
York Road
1973

-CCHS

Polish Easter Bread

Makes Four Loaves

Serve warm with dinner or enjoy as sandwich bread.

Dissolve the yeast and 1 teaspoon sugar in the water in a small bowl. In a large mixer bowl, combine scalded milk, butter and shortening. In another bowl, beat yolks with sugar and salt until lemony in color. When milk mixture is lukewarm, add 2 cups flour and beat well. Add yeast mixture and beat again. Add more flour beating well. Add yolk mixture and beat well. Gradually add remaining flour, kneading with hands until smooth and elastic, leaving hands clean. Cover and let rise in a warm place until double in size. Divide dough into 4 balls. Divide each ball into 3 strips for braiding. Braid each loaf and place into four 9x5" greased pans. Let rise for two hours. Preheat oven to 350°. Beat one egg and milk and brush the tops of the loaves. Bake at 350° for 35 to 40 minutes. Remove immediately from the oven and invert on to a wire rack. Brush the tops of the loaves with melted butter.

Cathy Belcher

- 2 packages dry yeast
- ¼ cup lukewarm water
- 1 teaspoon sugar
- ½ pound and 4 tablespoons butter
- 4 tablespoons Crisco
- 1 quart milk, scalded
- 6 large egg yolks
- ½ cup sugar
- 1 tablespoon salt
- 10 cups or more flour
- 1 egg
- 1 tablespoon milk
- melted butter

Raisin Pumpernickel Bread

Makes Two Loaves

This deserves real butter.

- 2 tablespoons dry yeast (2 packets)
- 2 cups warm water
- 1 teaspoon sugar or honey
- ¼ cup cider vinegar
- ⅓ cup dark molasses
- 6 tablespoons cocoa
- 2 tablespoons oil
- 1 scant tablespoon salt
- 1 tablespoon caraway seeds
- 1 teaspoon fennel seeds
- ½ cup raisins
- 3 cups white flour
- 3½ cups rye flour (or more)
- 2 tablespoons melted butter or margarine

Glaze
- ⅓ cup water
- 1 teaspoon corn starch

In a large mixer bowl, dissolve dry yeast and sugar in warm water. Add cider vinegar, molasses, cocoa, oil, salt, caraway seeds, fennel seeds, 3 cups white flour. Mix for 2 to 3 minutes. Stir in raisins. Add rye flour gradually while kneading with bread hook (or by hand on a floured surface). Knead 10 minutes. Let rise until doubled in size. Punch down and divide into two parts to form 2 oval loaves. Slash on the top with scissors. Brush with melted butter or margarine. Let rise until almost doubled. Bake in pre-heated 375° oven for 30 to 35 minutes. About 15 minutes before bread is done, make glaze by boiling ⅓ cup water and 1 teaspoon cornstarch. Brush glaze on loaves 10 minutes before bread is done.

Maureen Reed

Raisin Gems

Makes Two Dozen Muffins

Pour a cup of tea and enjoy these sweet, moist, spicy muffins.

Preheat oven to 325°. Cover raisins with water and simmer 20 minutes. Drain well, saving raisin juice. Cool raisins. Mix shortening, brown sugar, eggs, salt, vanilla and cinnamon together until light and fluffy. Add baking soda to raisin water (add cold water to make 1 cup if necessary). Alternating, add raisin water, raisins and flour to shortening/sugar mixture. Put into cupcake papers or greased muffin tins. Sprinkle with moist coconut and nuts. Top with half of a maraschino cherry. Bake for 30 minutes.

Frances Freet

- 1 pound dark seedless raisins
- ½ cup butter
- ½ cup margarine
- 2 cups or less light brown sugar
- 2 eggs
- 1 teaspoon salt
- 2 teaspoons vanilla
- 2 teaspoons cinnamon
- 3 cups flour
- 2 teaspoons baking soda

Topping
- coconut
- nuts
- maraschino cherries

Vienna Bread

Makes One Loaf

Serve as an hors d'oeuvre or along with a meal.

Preheat oven to 350°. Cut crisscrosses in bread. Stuff mushrooms, cheese and onions down in the cracks. Melt the butter and add the remaining ingredients to make a sauce. Pour the butter sauce slowly over the bread so that it seeps into the cracks. Seal in foil and bake for 25 to 30 minutes.

Peggy Adams

- 1 tablespoon Worcestershire sauce
- 1 cup butter (or less)
- 1 teaspoon dry mustard
- 2 teaspoons spicy seasoned salt
- ¼ cup minced onion
- 1 8 ounce can sliced mushrooms
- 2 cups shredded Swiss cheese
- 1 loaf baked bread (Italian store bought works well)

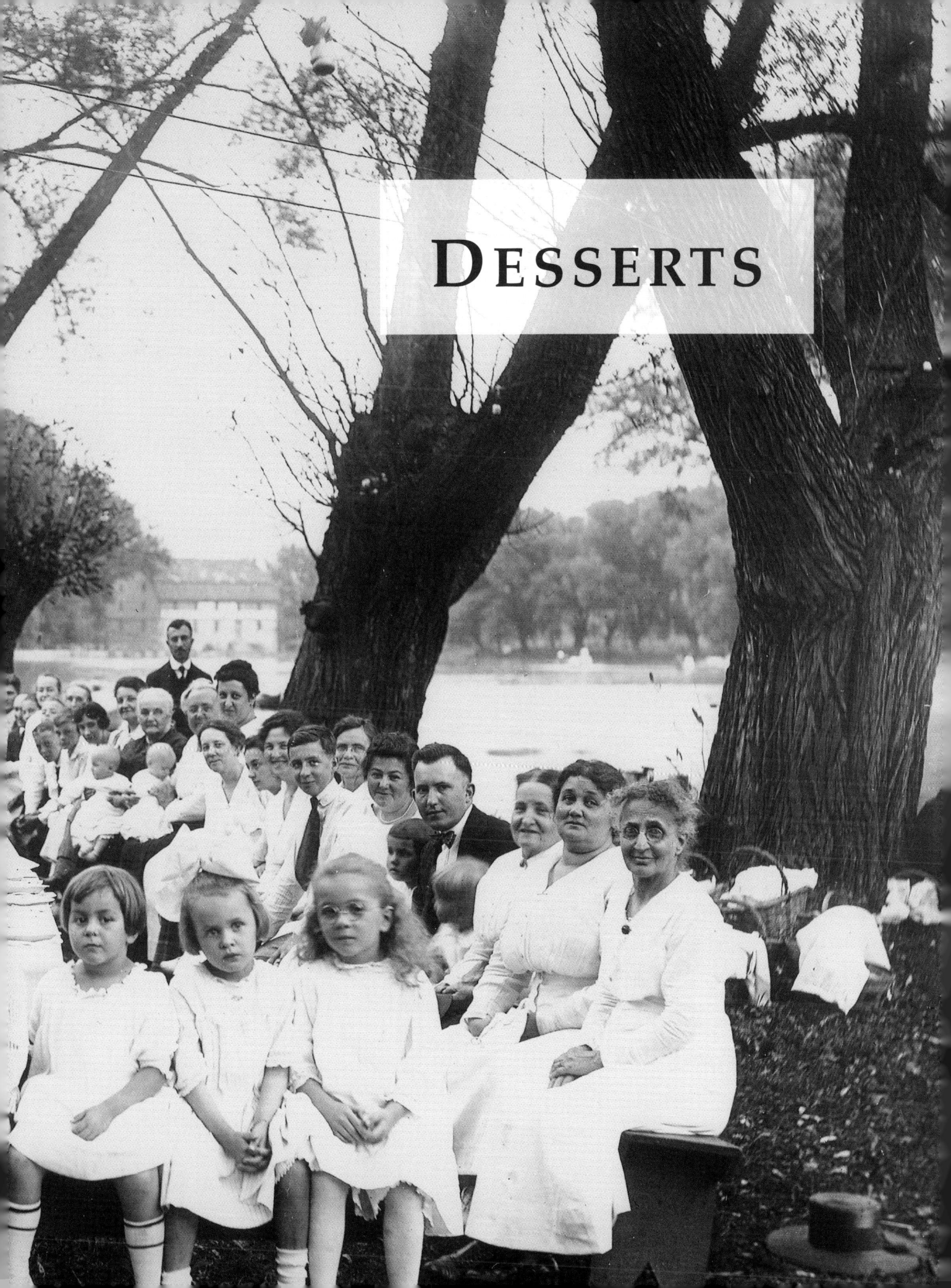
Desserts

APPLESAUCE CAKE

Serves Eight

Top with ice cream and enjoy.

- 1 cup sugar
- 1/2 cup butter
- 1 cup apple sauce
- 1 cup raisins
- 2 cups flour
- 1/2 teaspoon cinnamon
- 1/2 teaspoon cloves
- 1/2 teaspoon salt
- 1 teaspoon baking soda
- 4 tablespoons hot water

Preheat oven to 375°. Grease and flour an 8 inch square pan. Sift together flour, cinnamon, cloves, salt and set aside. Cream together sugar and butter. Add applesauce and raisins and beat well. Add flour mixture and beat well. Add baking soda which is dissolved in hot water. Beat well. Bake for 30 to 40 minutes or until toothpick comes out dry.

Elizabeth G. Minnich

SHOO FLY CUPCAKES

Makes Eighteen to Twenty-four

Pennsylvania Dutch Goodness.

- 2 1/2 cups flour
- 1/2 cup shortening
- 1 1/2 cups light brown sugar
- 1 cup brown sugar
- 1 teaspoon baking powder
- 1 teaspoon baking soda
- 1 1/2 cups boiling water

Preheat oven to 350°. Mix together flour, shortening and brown sugar. Save 1 cup of this mixture for top of cupcakes. Add rest of ingredients to above mixture. Spoon into lined muffin tins and top with crumbs. Sprinkle with cinnamon. Bake for 20 minutes.

Lorraine Humer

Jimmy Carter Cake

Serves Twelve to Sixteen

Layers of pudding, cream and peanuts, of course.

This cake is made in four layers.

FOR THE FIRST LAYER

Preheat oven to 350°. Mix together flour, margarine and chopped roasted peanuts. Press into a 9 X 13" pan. Bake for 20 minutes. Remove pan from oven and cool.

FOR THE SECOND LAYER

Cream the peanut butter and cream cheese. Add the sugar. Fold in the 1 cup Cool Whip. Spread over the cooled first layer.

FOR THE THIRD LAYER

Beat one package vanilla instant pudding and one package chocolate instant pudding with 2¾ cups milk. Pour over the second layer.

FOR THE FOURTH LAYER

Spread Cool Whip on top and garnish with chopped peanuts and shaved chocolate.
Keep refrigerated.

Blanche W. Myers

- 1 cup flour
- 1 stick margarine
- ⅔ cup dry roasted peanuts chopped
- ⅓ cup peanut butter
- 8 ounces cream cheese
- 1 cup confectioners sugar
- 1 cup Cool Whip
- 1 3 ounce package vanilla instant pudding
- 1 3 ounce package chocolate instant pudding
- 2¾ cups milk
- dry roasted chopped peanuts
- shaved chocolate
- Cool Whip for top of cake

Overleaf, **Goodyear Reunion**
Boiling Springs Park
August, 1919

-CCHS

CAKES 237

Carrot Cake

Serves Ten to Twelve

For a special occasion use two 8 or 9 inch cake pans and bake for 40 minutes. Ice with cream cheese frosting.

For the Cake

4	eggs beaten
½	cup oil
2	cups sugar
2	cups flour
¼	teaspoon salt
1½	teaspoons baking powder
1½	teaspoons baking soda
1	teaspoon cinnamon
1	teaspoon nutmeg
3	cups grated carrots

For the Frosting

1	8 ounce package cream cheese
¼	cup butter
2	cups sifted confectioners sugar
2	teaspoons vanilla

TO MAKE THE CAKE

Preheat oven to 350°. In a large bowl, beat eggs well. Add oil and sugar. Mix dry ingredients in a separate bowl. Add dry ingredients to egg mixture. Blend well. Add grated carrots. Blend well. Pour into an ungreased 9x13 inch pan. Bake for 50 minutes.

TO MAKE THE FROSTING

Beat together cream cheese and butter. Slowly beat in confectioners sugar and vanilla; beat until light and fluffy.

Mary Hock

Ad from The Shuttle Magazine
Masland Athletic Association
1927
Carlisle

-CCHS

Centerpiece Coconut Cake

Serves Twelve to Sixteen

This cake will turn any occasion into a celebration.

TO MAKE THE CAKE

Preheat oven to 350°. Sift flour once; measure. Add baking powder and salt and sift together 3 times. Cream butter thoroughly, add sugar gradually and cream together until light and fluffy. Beat egg yolks and add to creamed mixture. Add flour alternately with milk, a small amount at a time, beating after each addition until smooth. Add vanilla and coconut. Beat egg whites until stiff; fold into cake mixture quickly and thoroughly. Pour into two 9 inch greased and floured pans. Bake for 30 to 35 minutes or until cake tester comes out clean. Frost when cool.

TO MAKE THE FROSTING

Mix all ingredients in a large bowl, adding boiling water last. Beat to stiff peaks. Frost cake and sprinkle coconut over frosting. Store uncovered.

The Editors

Note
Keeps well in refrigerator for several days.

For the Cake
- 3 cups cake flour
- 2 teaspoons baking powder
- ¼ teaspoon salt
- 1 cup butter
- 1 1 pound box confectioners sugar
- 4 eggs, separated
- 1 cup milk
- 1 teaspoon vanilla
- 1 cup flaked coconut

For the Frosting
- 2 egg whites, unbeaten
- ½ teaspoon cream of tartar
- 2 teaspoons vanilla
- 1½ cups sugar
- ½ cup boiling water
- coconut

Aunt Katherine's Pound Cake

Makes One Large Bundt Cake

luscious lemon delicacy for pound cake lovers.

Cream butter, sugar, and shortening until sugar dissolves. Add eggs. Sift flour and baking powder together. Add flour and milk alternately. Add vanilla and lemon juice. Pour batter into a well greased and floured bundt or tube pan or two loaf pans. Place in cold oven, set at 325°. Cook 1½ hours (if using two loaf pans, 1 hour).

Jeanne Bowers

Note

The secret is to cover cake while still in pan and cool completely. This makes it "sweat" and hold moisture.

- 3 cups sugar
- 1 cup butter or margarine, softened
- ½ cup Crisco, heated to melting point
- 5 eggs, beaten
- 3 cups plain flour
- ½ teaspoon baking powder
- 1 cup milk
- 1 teaspoon vanilla
- 1 teaspoon lemon juice

Aunt Pearl's Lemon Cheese Icing

Ices One Large Bundt Cake

Frost Aunt Katherine's cake with this icing.

Mix and bring to a good boil, about 5 minutes. Cool and spread.

Jeanne Bowers

- 2 eggs
- 2 cups sugar
- 1 stick butter or margarine
- ¼ cup bottled lemon juice (or grated rind and juice of 2 large or 3 small lemons)

At left, **Parker House for Children**
    Carlisle
    c. 1920
    A. A. Line photographer
    -CCHS

Jonathan's Favorite Cake

Serves Ten to Twelve

Fat free, moist and delicious. No icing is needed.

- 2 cups sugar
- 1¾ cups flour (increase to 2 cups flour if applesauce is thin)
- ¾ cup cocoa
- 1½ teaspoons baking soda
- 1½ teaspoons baking powder
- 1 cup water
- ½ cup applesauce
- 2 teaspoons vanilla extract
- 3 egg whites
- 1 cup boiling water

Preheat oven to 350°. Combine first 6 dry ingredients and set aside. Combine 1 cup water, applesauce, vanilla and egg whites. Mix together dry ingredients with applesauce mixture. Add 1 cup boiling water to entire mixture, stirring gently to mix. Don't panic, mixture will be "runny." Pour into 13 X 9 inch pan that has been sprayed with no-stick cooking spray. Bake 20 to 30 minutes until center bounces back when tapped.

Wendy Weary Gambini

Date Nut Cake

Serves Eighteen to Twenty

This cake will keep for six weeks. You can keep this on hand for a quick dessert.

- 1 pound pitted dates
- 2 pounds English walnuts (1½ pounds if out of shell)
- 1 cup flour
- 1 cup granulated sugar
- 2 teaspoons baking powder
- 1 teaspoon vanilla
- 2 eggs
- 2 egg whites beaten until stiff

Preheat oven to 250°. Keep walnuts whole as they come out of shell. Cut dates in half. Pour sugar over dates, mix until coated. Combine flour, baking powder, whole eggs and mix. Add walnuts and dates. Fold in two beaten egg whites. Bake in greased bundt pan or two loaf pans for 2 hours.

Marjorie Dutrey

At right, **Church and Gleim Grocers**
Hanover and North Streets
Carlisle
c. 1910

-CCHS, Griffith Collection

St. Hubert's Irish Whiskey Cake

Serves Twelve to Sixteen

Additional ingredients could include the "twinkle of an eye from a young Irish colleen, the hardy laugh of a strapping Irish lad, and a fond mother's sigh."

TO MAKE THE CAKE

Preheat oven to 350°. Combine in mixer, cake mix and pudding mix. In separate bowl, mix milk, oil, and whiskey. Add eggs and walnuts. Add dry mixture and incorporate thoroughly. Pour into greased tube pan. Bake for 1 to 1½ hours.

TO MAKE THE GLAZE

Combine 1 tablespoon whiskey with remaining ingredients. Reserve other whiskey to end. Bring to boil and simmer for 10 minutes. Add remaining whiskey. Pour over cake before serving.

Hubert X. Gilroy

For the Cake

- 1   18 ounce box yellow cake mix
- 1   8 ounce box vanilla pudding mix
- ½ cup milk
- ½ cup oil
- 1   cup whiskey
- 4   eggs
- 1   cup chopped walnuts

For the Glaze

- 2   ounces sweet butter
- 1   tablespoon water
- 1   cup whiskey
- 1   cup sugar

KARITHOPETA

Serves Twelve to Sixteen

Greek Walnut Cake.

For the Cake

- 12 eggs, separated
- 4 cups walnuts, chopped (1 lb.)
- 2½ cups sugar
- 2 cups bread crumbs
- 1 teaspoon vanilla
- 1 tablespoon cinnamon

For the Syrup

- 2½ cups water
- 2½ cups sugar
- 1 teaspoon cinnamon
- few drops of lemon juice

TO MAKE THE CAKE

Preheat oven to 350°. Beat yolks until light in color. Add sugar, alternate bread crumbs and nuts (gradually). Add cinnamon and vanilla. Mixture will be very thick. Continue mixing with wooden spoon. Beat egg whites until stiff. Fold into nut mixture, mixing thoroughly with spoon. Pour into buttered pan, 11"x16". Bake about 45 minutes until brown.

TO MAKE THE SYRUP

In a saucepan, combine syrup ingredients. Boil about four minutes until syrupy. Set aside to cool. When cake is finished remove from oven and cut into diamond pieces while still hot. Immediately pour syrup over cake. Let cool before serving. Garnish with marachino cherry halves.

Louise Broujos

Walnuts

The 20th of June is the time to put up walnuts. Put them in salt one week; then take and scrape them. Put your vinegar over them cold, and spice and garlic.

Peachy Parker's Cookbook

Italian Creme Cake

Serves Eight to Ten

Luscious pecan cake with cream cheese frosting.

TO MAKE THE CAKE

Preheat oven to 350°. In large mixing bowl, beat margarine and shortening until combined. Add sugar; beat on medium-high speed until mixture is light and fluffy. Add egg yolks and vanilla; beat well. In another bowl, combine flour, baking powder and baking soda. Add to egg yolk mixture alternately with buttermilk, beating just until combined after each addition. Stir in coconut and chopped pecans. Wash beaters thoroughly. In a small mixing bowl, beat egg whites until stiff peaks form. Stir about ⅓ of the whites into the cake batter to lighten. Fold in remaining whites. Pour evenly into 3 greased and floured 8" cake pans. Bake for 25 to 30 minutes, until tops of layers are evenly golden and spring back when lightly pressed with a fingertip. Ice cooled layers with frosting. Refrigerate.

TO MAKE THE FROSTING

In small mixer bowl beat cream cheese, margarine or butter, and vanilla until smooth. Gradually add powdered sugar, beating until smooth. Keep half of the frosting nutless for the outside of the cake. Reserve half of the nuts to sprinkle on top of the cake.

Roberta March

For the Cake

- ½ cup butter or margarine, at room temperature, softened
- ⅓ cup shortening
- 1¾ cups sugar
- 4 eggs, separated
- 1 teaspoon vanilla
- 1¾ cups flour
- 1½ teaspoons baking powder
- ¼ teaspoon baking soda
- ¾ cup buttermilk
- 1 3½ ounce can flaked coconut
- 1 cup chopped pecans

For the Frosting

- 12 ounces cream cheese, room temperature
- 6 tablespoons butter or margarine, room temperature
- 1½ teaspoons vanilla
- 4 cups powdered sugar
- ½ cup chopped pecans

White Chocolate Fudge Cake

Serves Fourteen to Sixteen

White chocolate, pecans and coconut....a triple treat.

- 2½ cups flour
- ½ teaspoon baking powder
- 1 teaspoon baking soda
- ½ teaspoon salt
- ¾ cup or 6 ounces chopped or broken white chocolate
- ½ cup hot water
- 3 eggs
- 1½ cups sugar
- 1 cup unsalted butter or margarine
- 1 cup buttermilk combined with
- 1 teaspoon vanilla
- ½ cup chopped pecans

Preheat oven to 350°. Mix flour, baking powder, baking soda and salt together and set aside. In a small pan, melt white chocolate in hot water over low heat. Reserve. Separate eggs. Cream butter. Gradually, add sugar, cream well, and then add egg yolks, one at a time. Cream well. Add dry ingredients alternately with buttermilk. Add reserved melted chocolate. Fold in pecans and coconut. In a separate bowl, beat egg whites until they stand in peaks, add vanilla and fold into cake mixture. Bake in a greased bundt or angel food cake pan for 45 minutes or 2 nine inch round layer pans for 45 to 55 minutes, until top springs back when lightly pressed with fingertip and toothpick inserted near center comes out clean. Cool right side up on a rack. Serve with a light dusting of confectioners sugar.

Rosie Tregl

Velvet Cheese Cake

Serves Twelve

This extra creamy classic may be garnished with fresh berries.

Preheat oven to 300°. Mix crumbs and butter, and press into spring form pan. Beat cake ingredients until smooth. Pour cake ingredients over the crumb crust. Bake crust and cake for 30 minutes. Cool. Mix all topping ingredients together and spread on cooled cake. Return to oven and bake for 7 minutes at 450°. Remove and cool. Refrigerate for 4 hours before cutting.

Connie Krout

For the Crust
- 3/4 cup graham cracker crumbs
- 1/8 pound butter, melted

For the Cake
- 1 1/2 pounds cream cheese
- 3/4 cup sugar
- 1 teaspoon lemon juice
- 3 eggs
- 1/2 teaspoon vanilla with butternut

For the Topping
- 2 cups sour cream
- 1/2 cup sugar
- 1 teaspoon vanilla

Weights and Measures:

Butter the size of an egg = 1/4 cup
Butter the size of a walnut = 2 tablespoons
Coffee cup = 1 cup
Dash - 1/8 teaspoon
Dessert spoon = 1 1/2 teaspoons
Dram = 3/4 teaspoon
Drops, 60 = 3/4 teaspoon liquid
Gill = 1/2 cup
Lump = 2 tablespoons (of butter) Pinch = 1/8 teaspoon
Pint = 2 cups
Pound of eggs = 8 to 9 large (Colonial eggs were small, so cookbooks may suggest as many as 10 to 12 per pound)
Pound of flour = about 3 to 3 1/2 cups (This varies greatly, some sources specifying as much as 4 1/2 cups)
Pound of sugar = 2 to 2 1/2 cups
Quart = 2 pints
Salt spoon = 1/4 teaspoon
Scruple = 1/24 ounce (an apothecary weight: about 1/4 teaspoon)
Teacup = 3/4 cup
Tin cup = 1 cup
Tumblerful = 2 cups
Wineglass = 1/2 gill or 1/4 cup

Lorraine Luciano

At far left, **Carlisle Tea Company**
207 North Hanover Street
Carlisle
c. 1910

-CCHS, Griffith Collection

GINGERBREAD

Serves Fifteen

This recipe dates to the early 19th century, and is just as good today.

- ½ cup sugar
- ½ cup butter and shortening mixed
- 1½ teaspoons baking soda
- 1 teaspoon cinnamon
- 1 teaspoon ginger
- ½ teaspoon ground cloves
- ½ teaspoon salt
- 1 egg
- 1 cup Brer Rabbit Molasses
- 2½ cups sifted flour
- 1 cup hot water

Preheat oven to 350°. Cream shortening and sugar, add beaten egg, molasses, then dry ingredients which have been sifted together. Add hot water last, beat until smooth. Bake in 9 X 13" greased pan for 40 to 45 minutes.

Barbara Barnitz Lillich

War Cake

During the First World War years, when candied fruit was not available for the traditional fruit cake, Grandmother baked a War Cake. After the War ended and candied fruit was again available, the War Cake was preferred.

- 2 cups dark brown sugar
- 2 cups hot water
- 1 level teaspoon salt
- 2 tablespoons lard
- 1½ teaspoon cloves
- ½ teaspoon cinnamon
- 1 pound seeded raisins
- 1 cup of preferred nuts
- 3 cups flour
- 1 teaspoon baking soda

Mix first 8 ingredients in a kettle and let slowly boil for 5 minutes. When mixture is cold, add flour and baking soda. Place mixture into Angel Food cake pan. Preheat oven to 350° and bake for 1 hour. Test with toothpick. After cake cools, store in foil lined can for 1 month.

Wayne Rutz

PAST RECEIPTS PRESENT RECIPES

BANANA GINGERS

Makes Three to Four Dozen

If you have the special pan, the cookies look like bananas, otherwise, drop the dough on a cookie sheet.

Preheat oven to 350°. Cream sugar, molasses, shortening and egg. Add flour and buttermilk and spices, soda, salt, and cream of tartar. Mix well. Grease Banana Ginger pan and put 1 heaping teaspoon of mixture in both sides of the pan or drop by teaspoon on a greased cookie sheet. Bake for 10 minutes.

Pat Strickler

Note
When ready to serve, roll in confectioners sugar.

1¼	cups brown sugar
1¼	cups Brer Rabbit molasses (green label)
1¼	cups shortening
1	egg
1¼	cups buttermilk
1	teaspoon cinnamon
½	teaspoon ginger
1	teaspoon soda
½	teaspoon cream of tartar
½	teaspoon salt
4¼	cups flour (measure before sifting)

MARTHA WASHINGTON GINGER COOKIES

Makes Five to Six Dozen

Adapted from a recipe used by Martha Washington.

Preheat oven to 350°. Mix butter, shortening, sugar, beaten eggs and molasses together and beat well. Sift in dry ingredients until well-blended. Dough will be soft. Chill briefly (about 15 minutes). Form dough into 1" balls. Roll in extra granulated sugar, place on lightly greased cookie sheet and press lightly to flatten. Bake for 6 to 8 minutes. Do not over bake, as cookies will harden.

Carolyn Craig Osborn

¾	cup softened butter
¾	cup shortening
2½	cups granulated sugar
2	eggs, beaten
½	cup dark molasses
4	cups unbleached flour
2	teaspoons baking powder
2	teaspoons ground ginger
2	teaspoons cinnamon
2	teaspoons ground cloves

Moravian Ginger Cookies

Makes Six Dozen

What would Christmas be without the sweet smell of ginger?

- 1/2 cup plus 1 tablespoon brown sugar
- 3 tablespoons butter
- 3 tablespoons shortening
- 1 cup dark molasses
- 2 scant teaspoons baking soda
- 2 tablespoons boiling water
- 4 cups flour
- 1 3/4 teaspoons ginger
- 1 1/2 teaspoons ground cloves
- 1 1/2 teaspoons cinnamon

Melt butter and shortening and add to sugar in large bowl. Stir in molasses and the soda which has been dissolved in the boiling water. Combine spices with flour and gradually sift into butter and molasses mixture. Mix well. Form dough into log and wrap in waxed paper. Chill at least overnight to blend flavors. Preheat oven to 275°. When ready to roll, let the dough come to room temperature. Roll small portions of dough as thinly as possible directly onto a cookie sheet. Cut into shapes with cookie cutters and place entire sheet in freezer for several minutes to facilitate removing cookies to another cookie sheet for baking. Bake for 10 minutes.

Wendell Pass

Drop Sand Tarts

Makes Three Dozen

An easier recipe for a Pennsylvania favorite.

- 1 pound margarine or butter or half of each
- 2 cups sugar
- 3 eggs
- 3 1/2 cups sifted flour
- 2 teaspoons baking powder
- 2 teaspoons vanilla

Preheat oven to 350°. Cream margarine with sugar until light and fluffy. Add eggs and vanilla. Stir in flour and baking powder, mixing well. Drop by teaspoonful on ungreased cookie sheet. Bake until golden brown, about 6 or 7 minutes.

Karen Pasciullo

Sand Tarts

Makes Five Dozen

One hundred years old and still one of the most requested cookie recipes.

- 3 eggs
- 2 cups sugar
- 4 cups flour
- 1 cup butter
- 1 teaspoon baking soda
- 2 teaspoons cream of tartar

Preheat oven to 350°. Cream eggs, sugar, and butter. Gradually add dry ingredients. Roll very thin. May be cut into squares or diamonds. Bake for approximately 6 minutes. Don't let edges brown.

Reverend Frederick S. Weiser

Ebner Mentzer
Front Street, Boiling Springs
c. 1910

-Richard L. Tritt Collection

FILLED COOKIES

Makes Three to Four Dozen

So *good with a cold glass of milk.*

TO MAKE THE DOUGH
Sift together dry ingredients. Cream butter, sugar and salt. Add egg, milk and vanilla. Add dry ingredients, mix well. Dough will be sticky. Wrap in waxed paper and chill overnight.

TO MAKE THE FILLING
Mix sugar and flour in saucepan; add raisins, walnuts and juice. Heat and cook slowly until thick.

TO MAKE THE COOKIES
Preheat oven to 350°. Roll dough thin on a floured board and cut with a biscuit cutter. Place ½ teaspoon filling on circle, turn dough over to cover filling. Crimp edge with a fork. Bake on ungreased cookie sheet for 15 minutes.

Edna Kadel

Note
Make filling and dough one day ahead. Dough must be chilled overnight.

At left, **Boiling Springs Hotel**, side entrance
Center, Mr. and Mrs. Filler, Proprietors
c. 1880
J. N. Choate photographer

-CCHS, Eddy Collection

For the Cookie Dough
- ½ cup plus 2 tablespoons butter
- 1 cup sugar
- ½ teaspoon salt
- 1 egg, well beaten
- ½ cup milk, mixed with 1 teaspoon vinegar
- 1 teaspoon vanilla
- 3½ cups unsifted flour
- 2 teaspoons baking powder
- 1 teaspoon baking soda
- ½ teaspoon nutmeg

For the Filling
- 1 cup packed, ground raisins
- ½ cup ground walnuts
- ½ cup sugar
- 1 tablespoon flour
- ½ cup orange juice

DOUBLE QUICK DATE DESSERT

Makes Three Dozen

Wonderful served warm with ice cream.

- 1½ cups sifted flour
- 1 teaspoon soda
- ½ teaspoon salt
- 1 pound dates, cut in large pieces
- 1¼ cups sugar
- ¼ cup soft butter or margarine
- 1 cup boiling water
- 1 teaspoon vanilla
- ½ cup chopped walnuts

Preheat oven to 350°. Sift together flour, soda and salt. Set aside. In large bowl, combine dates, sugar, butter and boiling water. Blend well. Add dry ingredients, vanilla and chopped nuts. Mix well. Bake for 30 to 35 minutes in 9 X 13 inch pan, greased and floured on bottom only. Cut into squares and dust with powdered sugar.

Evelyn Rickert

AMAZING CRACKER CHUNKS

Makes Five Dozen

Tastes like toffee candy.

- 20-30 saltine crackers
- 1 cup butter (must use butter)
- 1 cup granulated sugar
- 1 12 ounce package semi-sweet chocolate chips

Preheat oven to 350°. Line cookie sheet with foil, making sure edges stand up at least ½". Arrange saltines in single layer to cover foil. Heat sugar and butter together, stirring until sugar is dissolved. Bring to a boil and boil 3 minutes. Pour sugar mixture over crackers on foil and bake 12 to 15 minutes. Remove from oven and immediately sprinkle with chocolate chips. When chocolate is melted, spread to cover candy mixture. Allow to cool. Break into chunks and store in airtight container in a cool place.

Peggy Wolf

GOBS

Makes Three Dozen

Miniature Whoopie Pies.

TO MAKE THE DOUGH

Preheat oven to 350°. Mix all ingredients in a large bowl, adding water last. Drop by teaspoon on to a greased cookie sheet. Bake about 15 minutes. Makes about 80 cookies. Put two cookies together with fluffy frosting.

TO MAKE THE FROSTING

Cook the milk and flour until thick. Set aside to cool. Mix together the sugar, shortening, vanilla and butter. Combine both mixtures and beat until fluffy. Put frosting between two cookies.

Nancy Wilson

For the Dough

- 1 cup butter or shortening
- 2 cups sugar
- 2 eggs
- 3 cups flour
- 1 cup cocoa
- 2 teaspoons baking soda
- 1 cup milk
- 1 teaspoon vanilla
- 1/2 cup hot water

For the Fluffy Frosting

- 1 cup milk
- 4 tablespoons flour
- 1 cup sugar
- 3/4 cup shortening
- 1 teaspoon vanilla
- 4 tablespoons butter

Sugar Bowl Candy Co.

Ice Cream

Soda Water

and

Home Made Candies

Wholesale and Retail

Harry Strophelus, Prop.

16 West Main Street

CARLISLE, PA.

Ad from **Farmers Directory of Cumberland County** *1914-1915*

-CCHS

COOKIES

BUTTER CRUNCH SQUARES

Makes Fifty-four Squares

Rich with nuts and cinnamon.

- 1 cup soft butter
- 1½ cups sugar
- 2 cups flour
- 1½ teaspoons cinnamon
- 1 egg yolk
- 2 egg whites
- 1 cup chopped walnuts

Preheat oven to 350°. Cream together butter and 1 cup of sugar. Add flour, 1 teaspoon cinnamon, and 1 egg yolk. Knead thoroughly and press dough lightly to ¼ inch thickness in 10 x 14 inch buttered baking pan. Brush 2 slightly beaten egg whites over dough. Sprinkle with mixture of ½ cup sugar and ½ teaspoon cinnamon and 1 cup of chopped nuts. Bake for 20 to 25 minutes. Cut into ½ inch squares while hot and cool in pan.

Bessie Jamieson

GRANDMA HARRIS' FROSTED CHEWIES

Makes Three Dozen Squares

Fancy version of Rice Krispy Squares.

- 1 cup sugar
- 1 cup light Karo syrup
- 1 cup peanut butter
- 6 cups Rice Krispies
- 1 cup chocolate chips
- 1 cup butterscotch chips

Cook sugar and corn syrup over medium heat until mixture boils. Remove from heat, add peanut butter, and pour over cereal in a large bowl. Mix well and press into greased 8x10 inch pan. Melt chips in a double boiler, and spread over cereal mixture. Cut into squares after it cools. Can store at room temperature or in refrigerator.

Ann Harris Roeder

At right, **Rakestraw's Ice Cream Plant**
South Market Street
Mechanicsburg
c. 1935

-Mechanicsburg Museum Association

256 PAST RECEIPTS PRESENT RECIPES

Grandma Shadeck's Ice Box Cookies

Makes Six Dozen

Another goodie from Grandma.

- 1 cup brown sugar
- 1 cup granulated sugar
- 1½ cups melted butter
- 3 eggs, unbeaten
- ¼ teaspoon salt
- 1 teaspoon cinnamon
- 2 teaspoons vanilla
- 4 cups flour
- 1 teaspoon baking soda
- 1 teaspoon cream of tartar
- 1 cup chopped nuts

Mix all ingredients together. Form into long logs and place on platter or cookie sheet. Cover and refrigerate overnight. Preheat oven to 325°. Slice crosswise as thin as possible. Bake for 10 to 12 minutes until edges are lightly browned.

Dena Shadeck Walker

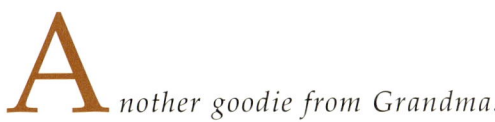

COOKIES 257

DIVINE DESSERT BARS

Makes Two Dozen

Bet you can't eat just one!!!

For the Crust
- 1/2 cup margarine, softened
- 1 cup flour
- 1/4 cup sugar

For the Filling
- 1 cup (approx. 10 squares) graham cracker crumbs
- 1/2 cup chocolate chips
- 1/2 cup chopped nuts
- 1 teaspoon baking powder
- 1/4 teaspoon salt
- 1 14 ounce can sweetened condensed milk

For the Frosting
- 1 1/2 cups confectioners sugar
- 1 teaspoon vanilla
- 1/2 cup margarine

Preheat oven to 350°. Lightly spoon flour into measuring cup; level off. In small bowl, cut margarine into flour and sugar until crumbly. Press in bottom of ungreased 8" square pan. Bake 10 minutes. Cool 10 minutes. In large bowl, combine all filling ingredients; mix well. Spread over partially baked crust. Return to oven and bake 15 or 20 minutes or until golden brown. Cool completely. In small bowl, blend all frosting ingredients until creamy. Spread over bars.

Carolyn Kenworthy

Note
For 9x13 inch pan, double recipe except frosting. May add a tiny bit of milk to make frosting more spreadable. Store in refrigerator for easier cutting.

At right, **Alice Moore Pours Coffee**
Two Mile House
South Middleton Township
c. 1910

-CCHS, Moore Collection

Nut Meringue Slices

Makes Sixty Bars

A delectable example of a European cookie, known as Hansi's Schnitten.

Preheat oven to 350°. In a bowl, using your hands, mix flour, sugar, butter and egg yolks. When the dough is smooth, pat it evenly over the bottom of a 10 x 15 inch jelly-roll pan. Prick the dough with a fork and bake for 15 to 20 minutes, or until pale gold. Remove from the oven, and spread jam over the surface. Beat egg whites until foamy, gradually add one cup sugar continuing to beat until very stiff. Fold in ground almonds or walnuts, and spread this nut meringue over the jam. Bake for 25 minutes, or until the top is golden. Cool in the pan, and cut into sixty 1 by 2½ inch bars.

Maria Bishop

2½ cups flour
½ cup sugar
½ pound sweet butter
2 egg yolks
1 cup raspberry jam, seedless

For the Topping
4 egg whites
1 cup sugar
1½ cups ground almonds or walnuts

Fudgelicious Brownies

Makes Three to Four Dozen

This one is for all the chocoholics.

For the Brownies

- 10 tablespoons butter
- 4 squares unsweetened chocolate
- 2 cups sugar
- 4 beaten eggs
- 1 teaspoon vanilla
- 1 1/2 cups flour
- 1/2 teaspoon salt

For the Fudge Frosting

- 3 cups powdered sugar
- 1/8 teaspoon salt
- 4 1/2 tablespoons cocoa
- 4 1/2 tablespoons softened butter
- 4 1/2 tablespoons strong coffee
- 3/4 teaspoon vanilla

TO MAKE THE BROWNIES

Preheat oven to 350°. Melt butter and chocolate together in double boiler. Remove and cool slightly. Add remaining ingredients. Pour into greased 9x13 inch pan. Bake for 30 minutes.

TO MAKE THE FROSTING

Sift dry ingredients into mixing bowl. Add butter, coffee and vanilla. Mix well. May add more coffee to achieve a smooth spreading consistency. Frost cooled brownies.

Chuck Wentzel

*At right, **A. Hock**
Newburg
July 8, 1909
Clyde A. Laughlin photographer*

-Shippensburg Historical Society Collection

ENGLISH BUTTER TOFFEE

Makes Two Pounds

T*his candy will keep for months if stored in an air tight container.*

Butter a 9x13 inch pan and spread almonds in the bottom. Butter a microwavable bowl. Put the rest of the butter in the bottom of the bowl. Carefully put sugar on top of the butter; avoid getting it on the sides of the bowl. Add salt and water. Cook in the microwave on high power until it becomes toffee-colored, about 14 to 15 minutes. Do not stir unless it appears to be dark in one "hot" spot. If you stir, be careful not to scrape the sides of the bowl or it may turn to sugar. As soon as the toffee syrup turns light tan-colored pour into the buttered almond pan. Any syrup scraped from the sides of the bowl may become sugary. When it starts to harden (a few minutes), score the top. When cool, break along the marks.

M. Susan Richman

1 cup butter
2 cups sugar
1 teaspoon salt
½ cup water
1 cup toasted almonds

DESSERTS 261

The Palace Confectionery Store
10 West High Street
Carlisle
c. 1950

-CCHS

Chocolate Almond Crunch

Makes One Pound

Fill pretty tins with this candy, and give as hostess gifts.

Lightly butter an 8x12 inch pan. In a heavy sauce pan, combine sugar, butter, water and salt. Cook over medium heat, stirring constantly until sugar is dissolved and mixture comes to a boil. Using a candy thermometer, cook to 290°. Remove from heat and quickly stir in ⅔ cup nuts. Pour into prepared pan immediately (it hardens very rapidly) and let cool. Melt chocolate and 1 tablespoon butter over very low heat. Mix well and spread over cooled candy. Sprinkle with remaining nuts and press lightly into soft chocolate. Refrigerate until chocolate hardens. Break into pieces and store in an airtight container in a cool place.

1	cup sugar
½	cup butter
3	tablespoons water
¼	teaspoon salt
1	cup finely chopped, toasted almonds
8	ounces semisweet chocolate
1	tablespoon butter

Peggy Wolf

Peanut Butter Easter Eggs

Makes Four Dozen Medium Sized Eggs

The Rice Krispies lighten the texture of this holiday favorite.

Mix together with your hands the peanut butter, Rice Krispies, and sugar and soft margarine until the Rice Krispies crunch. Shape into an egg shape on a teaspoon or tablespoon depending on the size you prefer. Meanwhile in the top of a double boiler, melt the paraffin and chocolate until smooth. Dip the eggs into the chocolate and cool them on wax paper. Dip pretzels into any remaining chocolate for more treats.

1	pound confectioners sugar
2	cups creamy peanut butter
3	cups Rice Krispies
¼	pound soft margarine
2	7-ounce Hershey chocolate bars
½	4-ounce bar paraffin

Linda Mohler Humes

No Fail Fudge

Makes Five Dozen

By following the directions, this is a fail proof recipe.

- 1 small can evaporated milk
- 16 large marshmallows
- 1⅓ cups sugar
- dash of salt
- ¼ cup butter
- 1½ cups chocolate chips
- 1 teaspoon vanilla
- 1 cup chopped walnuts, optional

Mix milk, marshmallows, sugar, salt and butter in a heavy saucepan. Stirring constantly, heat to boiling, and boil 5 minutes. Remove from heat. Add chocolate chips and stir until melted. Stir in vanilla and walnuts. Spread in a buttered 8 inch pan. Cut when cooled.

Anita Zimmerman

Note

This fudge recipe won't fail as long as you keep stirring the whole time. If you stop or remove from heat too soon, it will be sugary.

Menu Cover
The Natty Nook
146 South Hanover Street
1930

-CCHS

Graham Cracker Roll

Serves Eight to Ten

A unique "no bake" treat.

Roll crackers fine. Cut marshmallows and dates in small pieces. Chop walnuts fine. In a large bowl, mix all with whipped cream and form into a roll, covering with a few extra cracker crumbs. Wrap in waxed paper and let stand overnight in refrigerator. Cut in slices, garnish with whipped cream.

Marjorie Katzman

- ½ pound graham crackers (or 2 cups)
- ½ pound marshmallows
- ½ pound dates
- ½ pound walnuts
- ½ pint whipping cream (whipped) and extra for garnish

Gram's Apple Surprise

Serves Eight

An easy dessert, reminiscent of apple crisp.

Preheat oven to 375°. Combine applesauce and raisins. Place in a greased baking dish. Put marshmallows on top of apple mixture. Melt butter in skillet and add bread crumbs and blend. Add sugar, nuts and cinnamon, mixing well into bread crumbs. Spread this mixture over marshmallow layer. Bake for 25 minutes.

Marguerite E. Grove

- 2 cups applesauce
- ¾ cup raisins
- ½-1 cup miniature marshmallows
- 2 teaspoons butter
- 1 teaspoon cinnamon
- 1¾ cups dry bread crumbs
- 1 cup brown sugar
- ½ cup chopped nuts

Baked Apple Alaska

Serves Six to Eight

Present this beautiful dessert at the table, and spoon into individual dishes for a show stopper ending.

- 4 cups cored, peeled, and sliced apples
- ½ cup seedless golden raisins
- ¼ cup water
- ½ cup firmly packed brown sugar
- 1 teaspoon cinnamon
- ½ teaspoon mace
- 3 egg whites
- 6 tablespoons sugar
- 1 pint firm vanilla ice cream

Preheat oven to 350°. Combine apples and raisins in a one and one half quart baking dish. Sprinkle with water. Combine brown sugar and spices, and spoon over the apples. Bake for 35 minutes, or until apples are soft, stirring occasionally. Let cool, then chill. Just before serving time, beat the egg whites until stiff. Add sugar gradually while continuing to beat until very stiff and glossy. Spoon ice cream over apples. Top with deep swirls of meringue, being careful to bring meringue to edge of dish. Bake in pre-heated oven at 450° for 3 to 4 minutes until meringue is tipped with brown.

Sue Horner Reed

At right, **Menu Cover** *Diana Sweet Shop Mechanicsburg*

-CCHS

At left, **Ad from the Farmer's Directory of Cumberland County 1914-1915**

-CCHS

Apples Peaches and Grapes

If you are looking for fine fruit of the highest quality and color, take a day off and visit

Leonard's Fruit Farm

three miles North of Kingstown, R. R. No. 1, or call on the Independent Telephone (Mechanicsburg 173-3), and have our fruit wagon bring you a sample. You can also find us each Wednesday at Stall No. 14 Broad Street Market, Harrisburg, and Saturday at Carlisle Market House.

F. E. LEONARD

New Kingstown, Pa., R. R. No. 1

Cinnamon Apples

Serves Eight

Welcome the apple season with this easy to prepare dessert.

Preheat oven to 350°. Cook the first three ingredients until cinnamon candies are dissolved. Place apples in a large baking dish and pour syrup over apples. Bake for 45 minutes, (or until apples are tender) basting occassionally. When cool serve with whipped cream and chopped nuts.

Marianne Fry

- 2 cups granulated sugar
- 2 cups water
- 1 cup cinnamon heart candies
- 8 baking apples, pared and cored
-   whipped cream
-   chopped nuts

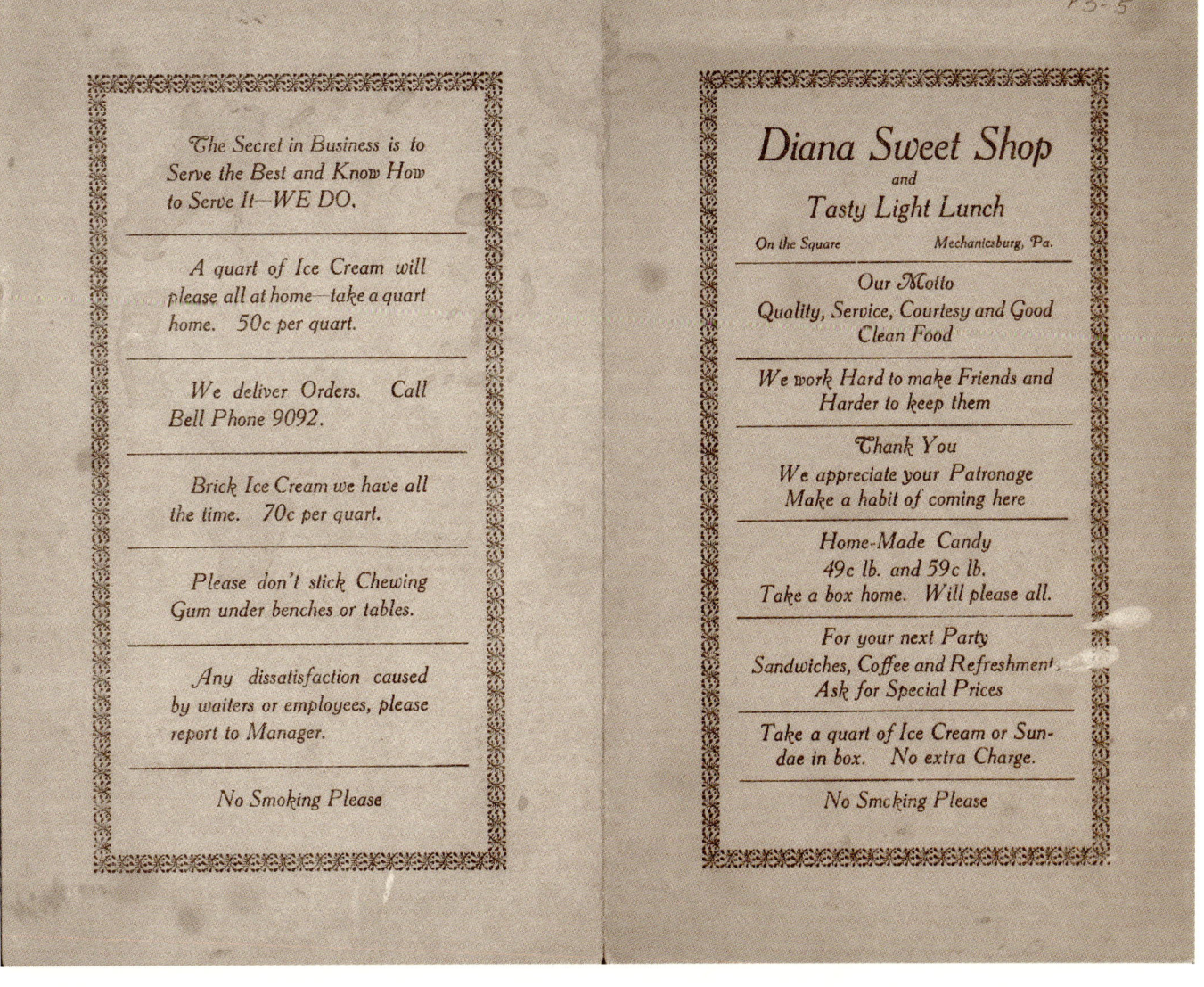

Lemon Sponge Pudding

Serves Eight

One of the Judge's favorite recipes from his mother.

- 1 cup sugar
- ¼ cup flour
- ⅛ teaspoon salt
- 2 tablespoons butter
- 4-5 tablespoons lemon juice
- 1 teaspoon grated lemon peel
- 2 well beaten egg yolks
- 1 cup milk, scalded
- 2 egg whites, beaten until stiff

Preheat oven to 325°. Combine sugar, flour, salt and butter. Add lemon juice and grated peel. Stir in egg yolks, and milk. Mix. Fold in egg whites. Pour in greased 1½ quart baking dish. Bake in a pan of hot water for 1 hour.

George Hoffer

Baked Rice Pudding

Serves Ten to Twelve

Serve this warm or cold with whipped cream.

- 1 cup minute rice, cooked according to package directions
- ¾ cup sugar
- 2 tablespoons butter
- 4 eggs
- ½ tablespoon cinnamon
- 2 dashes nutmeg
- 2 12 ounce cans evaporated milk
- 1 cup regular milk
-   raisins, optional

Butter a 2½ quart casserole dish, and preheat the oven to 350°. Cream and mix sugar, butter, eggs and spices. Add milk and then rice to mixture. Pour into casserole dish. Bake uncovered 45 to 55 minutes.

Dave Witmer

Note
To add raisins, plump in hot water, drain and stir into rice mixture before baking.

Black and White Bread Pudding

Serves Eight

 glorious ending to a special evening at the Global Empire Cuisine.

TO MAKE THE PUDDING

Combine half and half with bittersweet chocolate in small saucepan and heat over low, stirring until chocolate melts. Combine sugar, eggs, yolk and vanilla in a large metal bowl and whisk until pale ribbons form. Add chocolate and half and half mixture and whisk to combine. Pour over bread cubes and allow to soak for at least 30 minutes, then add white chocolate chunks and stir to mix. Spoon mixture into buttered ramekins and bake in a water bath at 350° for 35 to 45 minutes, or until they spring back when touched. Run a knife around sides and invert. Garnish with white chocolate curls. Top with Espresso Creme Anglaise. Can be prepared ahead and reheated in a covered water bath.

TO MAKE THE CREME ANGLAISE

In a small sauce pan, scald milk. Slowly stir in whisked yolks and sugar. Do not allow to boil! Stir constantly until it begins to thicken. As it cools, beat it to release the steam. Before chilling, add espresso. Chill for at least 4 hours. Pour over bread pudding.

Caroline Bogar

For the Bread Pudding

- 3 cups half and half
- 8 ounces bitter sweet chocolate, chopped roughly
- 2 cups sugar
- 3 whole eggs
- 1 egg yolk
- 1 tablespoon vanilla
- 1 loaf white bread, cut into ½ inch cubes
- 4 ounces white chocolate, chopped roughly

For the Espresso Creme Anglaise

- 1½ cups milk
- 6 slightly beaten egg yolks
- ½ cup plus 2 tablespoons sugar
- ⅛ teaspoon salt
- 1 tablespoon strong espresso

Spanish Cream

Serves Four to Six

Mold this classic dessert or serve in elegant individual dishes.

- 1 envelope Knox gelatin
- 3 cups milk
- ½ cup sugar or ¾ cup light corn syrup
- 3 eggs, separated, whites beaten until stiff
- ½ teaspoon salt
- 1 teaspoon vanilla

Soften gelatin in ¼ cup of cold milk. Beat yolks, add remaining milk, corn syrup (or sugar) and salt. Cook in double boiler until of custard consistency, stirring constantly. Add softened gelatin and stir until dissolved. Remove from stove and fold in vanilla and stiffly beaten egg whites. Turn into one large or individual molds, which have been rinsed in cold water first and chilled.

Elizabeth Masland

Rhubarb Tapioca Pudding

Serves Eight

From the kitchen of my great grandmother, a delicious treat.

- 2 cups water
- ⅓ cup minute tapioca
- ½ teaspoon salt
- 1¼ cups sugar
- 2½ cups rhubarb, chopped
- 1 cup fresh pineapple, peeled, sliced thinly and shredded whipped cream

Place water in top of double boiler and bring to a boil over direct heat. Combine minute tapioca, salt, sugar and rhubarb. Add to water and bring to a brisk boil, stirring constantly. Place over rapidly boiling water in bottom of double boiler and cook 5 minutes, stirring occasionally until rhubarb is cooked (it will partially break up). Remove from heat and cool. When almost cool, fold in pineapple. Chill and serve with whipped cream.

Sondra Wolfe Elias

At right, **Franklin Grocery Store**
29 South Hanover Street
Carlisle
c. 1915

-CCHS

Raspberry-Brownie Ice Cream Cake

Serves Eight to Ten

You may substitute your favorite brownie recipe or use a brownie mix for these brownies. Try serving this recipe in parfait dishes or use different combinations of ice cream, sherbet and fruit.

For the Brownies

- 4 ounces semisweet chocolate, chopped
- 6 tablespoons unsalted butter
- 9 tablespoons plus 1 teaspoon all purpose flour
- 1/2 teaspoon baking powder
- pinch of salt
- 1 cup sugar
- 1 teaspoon vanilla
- 2/3 cup walnuts, coarsely chopped

For the Filling

- 1 pint raspberry sherbet
- 2 1/2 cups vanilla ice cream

For the Topping

- 1 cup whipping cream, well chilled
- 2 teaspoons sugar
- 1 teaspoon vanilla
- fresh raspberries

TO MAKE THE BROWNIES

Position rack in center of oven and preheat to 350°. Line an 8-inch square pan with parchment or foil; butter paper or foil. Melt chocolate and 3 tablespoons butter in double boiler over hot, but not boiling water. Stir until smooth. Cool slightly. Sift flour, baking powder and salt together. Blend egg and sugar. Mix in vanilla. Gradually beat in chocolate mixture. Stir in dry ingredients, then walnuts. Spread batter evenly in prepared pan. Bake until tester comes out dry, about 19 minutes. Cool completely; invert onto rack and remove paper or foil. Cut into 16 squares. Freeze brownies until firm, but not solid, about 2 hours. Line bottom of 8-inch square pan with waxed paper. Freeze about 15 minutes. To fill, soften sherbet in refrigerator until spreadable. Smooth into prepared pan. Freeze until firm, about 15 minutes. Soften 1 cup of ice cream until spreadable. Smooth over sherbet. Freeze until firm. Cut each brownie into 3 layers. Cover ice cream with half of brownies, pressing slightly into ice cream. Freeze until firm, about 15 minutes. Soften remaining 1 1/2 cups ice cream and spread over brownies. Freeze 15 minutes. Cover ice cream with remaining brownies. Press into ice cream. Cover and freeze for 8 hours or overnight. Run knife around edges of brownie pan and invert onto platter; peel off parchment or foil. Return to freezer.

TO MAKE THE TOPPING

Whip cream with sugar and vanilla. Top each cake with whipped cream and a fresh raspberry.

Susan Fritschler

Tart Tatin

Serves Eight

A heavenly apple tart.....baked upside down.

TO MAKE PASTRY

Make sure all ingredients are at room temperature. Mix all ingredients in a bowl by hand until you have a smooth ball. Refrigerate at least 20 minutes or up to a week.

TO MAKE THE FILLING

Preheat oven to 400°. Peel apples and cut them coarsely, three to four chunks per seeded apple quarter. In a thick or non-stick frying pan, melt butter gently. Add sugar and apples and turn the heat to high. Stir often. Turn heat down if sugar starts coloring too early, up if juice starts accumulating. After about 10 minutes, the apples should be the color of perfect fried potatoes, in a thick golden syrup. Transfer to an ungreased 10 inch glass pie plate. Roll out the pastry and place on top of the apples. Tuck a bit around the apples. Trim any overhang. Bake for 15 minutes. Give the pie a half turn and bake for 15 minutes more (total of 30 minutes). Let stand a minute or so, cover with a serving plate and quickly but carefully, invert without burning yourself. Remove pie plate carefully, repositioning any stray apple chunks. Serve warm.

Oliver Hazan

For the Pastry

1	egg
1	tablespoon water
1	tablespoon sugar
1¾	cups flour
10	tablespoons butter

For the Filling

8	apples (about 2½ pounds)
8	tablespoons butter
¾	cup and 2 tablespoons sugar

YOUR HEALTH DEMANDS
ICE TWELVE MONTHS
IN THE YEAR
Carlisle Hygienic Ice Co.
FOOT OF LOUTHER STREET
24 Hour Service at Plant—Day & Night
Both Phones

Ad from the Shuttle Magazine
Masland Athletic Association
1927
Carlisle

-CCHS

Deluxe Apple Pie

Makes One Nine Inch Pie

An American tradition, apple and ice cream.

- ½ cup water
- 2 tablespoons cornstarch
- ¾ cup sugar
- ½ teaspoon cinnamon
- 1 tablespoon butter
- 1 quart fresh apples
- 1 9 inch unbaked pie shell

Preheat oven to 375°. Prepare pie shell. Peel and slice apples, place in pie shell. Bring water and cornstarch to a boil and cook slowly until thick and clear. Stir in sugar, cinnamon, and butter, and bring to a boil. Remove from the heat and pour over apples. Bake 35-40 minutes, or until crust is golden brown.

Janet Hocker

GRANDMOTHER'S BLACK RASPBERRY PIE

Serves Eight

You can have raspberry pies all year long if you buy the berries in season and freeze them. When purchased, pick them over and remove all stems and leaves, but do not wash them. Put into one quart bags and freeze. When you are ready to make a pie take a bag out of the freezer and thaw; it is not necessary to thaw the raspberries completely to use them.

Preheat oven to 450°. Put 2 cups flour into a bowl. Add the cold margarine which has been cut into pieces and work it into the flour with a pastry cutter. When the flour and butter are blended so that there are no clumps larger than a pea, it is ready for the next step. Break one egg into a bowl, and with a fork beat with one tablespoon of water. (This whole mixture will not be used.) Fill a ¼ measuring cup with the egg/water mixture and add this to the flour/butter mixture. Work the liquid into the mixture (fingers work better than a fork). This step should only take about a minute until the dough is ready. Divide dough into two pieces. Spread two overlapping sheets of waxed paper on the counter. Take one portion of dough and put it in the middle of the paper. Flatten the ball into a small circle and then cover with two more overlapping sheets of waxed paper. Roll the dough between the sheets of paper, turning as you roll to make a neat circle. When the dough is rolled out, peel the waxed paper from the top. With the waxed paper still attached to the bottom of the dough, place face down over the pie plate and peel off the waxed paper. Lightly fit the dough into the pie plate. Mix the raspberries, sugar, tapioca granules and salt. Pour into the pie shell. Roll out the remaining dough and place it on the top of the pie. Press the uneven edges of the top and bottom pie dough together then turn under to make a neat circle along the rim of the pie plate. Crimp edge. Pierce the top crust with a fork. Place the pie into a preheated oven for 15 minutes. Open the oven door for one minute to cool down the oven and turn the temperature down to 350°. Bake for 35 minutes more. Place the pie on a rack to cool. Cool for several hours before serving.

Merri Lou Schaumann

For the Crust
- 2 cups flour
- ⅔ cup plus 2 tablespoons margarine or butter (do not use "light" or substitute)
- 1 egg
- water
- waxed paper
- 9" pie plate

For the Pie
- 1 quart black raspberries
- 1 cup sugar
- 2 tablespoons minute tapioca (granules)
- pinch of salt

At left, **Carlisle Farmers Market**
York Road
c. 1960

-CCHS

Fruit Cream Pie

Makes One Ten-inch Pie

A delectable tropical fruit filling.

For the Crust
- 1½ cups vanilla wafers, crushed
- ¼ teaspoon melted butter or margarine

For the Pie
- 1 can Eagle brand milk
- ½ cup lemon juice (bottled)
- 1 cup mandarin oranges (small can), drained
- 1 cup pineapple chunks (small can), drained
- ½ cup coconut
- ½ cup pecans, chopped
- ½ cup whipping cream, whipped confectioners sugar (to sweeten whipping cream)

TO MAKE THE CRUST

Preheat oven to 400°. Mix the crust ingredients together and press firmly into a 10 inch pie pan, saving a few crumbs for the top of the pie. Bake for 5 minutes.

TO MAKE THE PIE

Mix milk and lemon juice thoroughly with spoon. Fold in drained fruits and nuts and coconut. Turn into crumb crust. Top with whipped cream - spread cream to edges of pie crust. Sprinkle crumbs on top. Refrigerate at least 6 hours.

Emmy Robbins Stuart

Jay Cooke, the financier who once owned Pine Grove Furnace, brought his cronies there on trout fishing trips. They loved this pie made by Margaret Tawser Weiser (1816-1896).

Cream Pie

Baked rich pie shell, cooled
Cream, to size of pie shell
Vanilla and sugar to taste
Currant jelly, as needed

Beat or whip the cream stiff. Add vanilla and sugar to taste. Fill pie shell. Dot with currant jelly.

Rev. Frederick S. Weiser

Grapefruit Pie

Serves Eight

Capture the attention of your guests when you serve this fabulous pie.

Prepare and bake a 9 inch pie shell. Cool. Drain 2 cans grapefruit sections and reserve juice. Melt the 32 marshmallows, dash of salt and hot water in a double boiler. Cool, then add ¼ cup reserved juice. When partially set, add grapefruit sections. Pour into prepared pie shell. Spread whipped cream over top of the pie and sprinkle with toasted coconut. Chill several hours before serving.

Thora Schroeder

- 1 pie shell
- 2 cups canned grapefruit sections, drained
- 32 marshmallows
- dash salt
- ¼ cup hot water
- ¾ cup whipping cream
- ¼ cup flaked coconut, toasted

Aunt Ruth's Lemon Sponge Pie

Serves Six

A tart creamy ending.

Preheat oven to 325°. Mix the sugar, flour, butter, lemon juice and egg yolks. Add milk. Fold in egg whites, beaten stiff. Pour mixture into pie shell and bake for 45 minutes.

Susan Starr

- 1 pie shell
- 1 cup sugar
- 2 tablespoons flour
- 2 tablespoons melted butter
- juice of 1 lemon
- 2 eggs
- 1 cup milk

Buttermilk Coconut Custard Pie

Makes One Nine Inch Pie

Forget about the calories, this is worth it.

- ½ cup melted butter (not margarine)
- 3 beaten eggs
- ½ cup buttermilk
- 1¼ cups sugar
- 2 tablespoons flour
- 1 teaspoon vanilla
- 1 can (3½ ounces) flaked coconut, divided
- 1 unbaked pie shell

Preheat oven to 325°. Combine the butter, eggs and buttermilk. Mix well. Add the sugar and flour. Mix. Add the vanilla, and ⅔ of the coconut. Pour into pie shell. Sprinkle with the remaining coconut. Bake for 65 minutes.

Deborah K. Westbrook

Fresh Peach Meringue Pie

Makes One Nine Inch Pie

With its cloud-high, golden tinged meringue, this peach pie is a Blue Ribbon winner.

TO MAKE THE PIE CRUST

Mix flour and salt in a medium bowl. Cut shortening into flour mixture until mixed. Add milk to form soft ball. Roll out onto a floured surface until size of 9" pie tin. Loosen dough from surface with knife and place in pie pan. Pinch edges of dough into pie pan.

TO MAKE THE PIE

Preheat oven to 450°. For pie, slice enough peeled peaches to fill pie pan. Mix flour and sugar, add melted butter and beaten egg yolks. Form a smooth mixture. Spoon evenly over peaches. Bake pie, without meringue, for 5 to 10 minutes on the bottom shelf until crust begins to brown. Then turn down oven to 325° and bake until peaches are soft 30 to 40 minutes. Remove pie from oven, spread meringue on peaches to edge of pie crust and bake at 325° until meringue is slightly brown, 10 to 15 minutes.

TO MAKE THE MERINGUE

Beat egg whites until stiff. Gradually add sugar. Beat after each addition.

Betty Parsell

Note
Add a little more flour if peaches are very juicy.

For the Pie Crust
1 cup flour
1 teaspoon salt
1/3 cup shortening
3 tablespoons milk

For the Filling
4-6 ripe peaches, peeled
1 cup sugar
2 tablespoons flour
2 tablespoons butter, melted
2 egg yolks, beaten

For the Meringue
2 egg whites
1/4 cup sugar
(double for a higher meringue)

At left, **Kenneth Steck Asleep In His Grandfather's Peach Orchard**
An August afternoon, 1897
Cumberland County

-Mr. and Mrs. Pierson K. Miller Collection

Pies 279

Homestead Raisin Pie

Makes One Nine Inch Pie

This old fashioned favorite is often found at country auction food stands.

For the Pie

- 1½ cups seeded raisins
- 2 cups water
- 3 eggs separated
- 1 cup sugar
- 2 tablespoons vinegar
- 2 tablespoons flour
- 2 tablespoons butter
- 3 egg whites
- 1 9 inch pie shell

For the Meringue

- 3 egg whites
- ¼ teaspoon cream of tartar
- 6 tablespoons sugar

Preheat oven to 350°. Add raisins to water in saucepan and simmer five minutes. Beat egg yolks, sugar, vinegar and flour until light and creamy. Slowly add to raisins. Cook, stirring constantly until filling is thick. Remove from heat, stir in butter and cool until luke warm. Pour raisin mixture into pie shell and top with meringue. Bake until meringue is brown, approximately 12 to 15 minutes.

TO MAKE MERINGUE

Beat egg whites until light and frothy. Add cream of tartar and beat until the whites are stiff enough to hold a peak. Gradually add the sugar and beat until the meringue is glossy. Spread the meringue on pie filling, touching the edges of the crust to prevent shrinkage.

Ruth Heberlig

At right, East High Street between Hanover and Bedford Streets
Carlisle
c. 1900
A. A. Line photographer

-CCHS

Sweet Potato Pie
Serves Eight

T*he fourth floor of the Cumberland County Court House rates this pie a winner.*

Preheat oven to 350°. Boil sweet potatoes until tender. Peel, mash or beat. Add butter, sugar, spices, and salt and mix into sweet potatoes. Add egg, vanilla, milk and beat until creamy. Spoon into pie shell. Bake for 50 to 60 minutes.

Sara Crawley Marshall

Note
Can be placed in a greased baking dish and topped with crushed cinnamon graham crackers or minature marshmallows.

- 3-4 medium sweet potatoes
- 6 tablespoons melted butter
- 1 cup sugar
- ¾ teaspoon pumpkin pie spice
- dash of salt
- 1 beaten egg
- 1 teaspoon vanilla
- 1 cup evaporated milk
- 1 unbaked 9 inch pie shell

Pecan Pumpkin Pie

Makes One Eight Inch Pie

 *traditional Thanksgiving recipe with a crunch.*

- 3 eggs
- 1 cup cooked mashed pumpkin
- ⅔ cup sugar
- ½ cup corn syrup
- 1 cup pecan halves
- 1 teaspoon milk
- 1 teaspoon cinnamon
- ½ teaspoon salt
- 1 unbaked pie shell

Preheat oven to 450°. Mix all ingredients. Pour into an 8 inch unbaked pie shell. Bake for 12 minutes at 450° and then at 350° for 35 minutes until knife comes out clean when tested.

Deborah K. Westbrook

Kahlua Pecan Pie

Makes One Nine Inch Pie

 *taste of Mexico in a rich pecan pie.*

- 1 pie shell
- ¼ cup butter
- ¾ cup sugar
- 1 teaspoon vanilla
- 2 tablespoons flour
- 3 eggs
- ½ cup Kahlua with ½ to 1 teaspoon instant coffee added
- ½ cup dark corn syrup
- ¾ cup evaporated milk
- 1 cup whole or chopped pecans
- ½ cup heavy cream, whipped

Line 9-inch pie plate with your favorite pastry recipe. Chill. Preheat oven to 400°. Cream together butter, sugar, vanilla, flour. Mix well. Beat in eggs, one at a time. Stir in Kahlua, corn syrup, evaporated milk, pecans. Mix well but do not whisk, as air incorporated at this stage will cause the pie to crack when cooling. Pour into pie shell. Bake for 10 minutes, then reduce heat to 325° and bake until firm (about 40 minutes). Chill and when ready to serve, garnish with whipped cream and pecan halves.

Virginia Schweiter

A Gooey Shoo Fly Pie

Makes Two Nine Inch Pies

Purchased at a summer yard sale, this pie was such a hit that the recipe was tracked down the same day!

Beat syrups, light brown sugar and eggs together. Dissolve baking soda in hot water and add to first mixture. Stir well. Mix ingredients for crumbs together and mix with hands until nice and crumbly. Pour 1 cup of syrup into each unbaked pie shell. Sprinkle handful of crumbs over the top. Pour rest of syrup into pie shells and top with remaining crumbs. Place pies into oven and set at 400°. <u>Do not preheat oven.</u> Bake 10 minutes. Reduce to 350° and bake for 30 minutes.

Minnie Kramer,
grandmother of
Martha Heberleigh

- 2 nine inch pie shells
- 1½ cups King syrup
- ½ cup Brer Rabbit (dark) syrup
- ½ cup light brown sugar
- 2 eggs
- 1 teaspoon baking soda
- 1½ cups hot water

For the Crumbs
- 2½ cups flour
- 1 cup light brown sugar
- ½ cup Crisco
- dash salt

Homemade Soap

Dissolve 2 cans lye in 7 pints cold water. Add 10 pounds luke-warm grease. Stir well. Add ½ pound borax and mix thoroughly. Mix in 2 cups Linso or other suds. Stir until set. Use a large crock or granite dish pan.

Two Mile House

Mince Meat Pie

Makes Five Pies

All of Fredith Shaw's family and friends love her mince meat pie, even if they don't like mince meat. A hunter relative who bags a deer in the fall always provides her with the neck meat. Everyone looks forward to mince meat pies at Thanksgiving and Christmas.

- 4 cups ground cooked meat, beef or venison (neck meat)
- 10 cups tart apples
- 2 pounds raisins
- 4 cups brown sugar
- ½ teaspoon ground cloves
- 1¼ teaspoons nutmeg
- 1½ teaspoons cinnamon
- 1 teaspoon ginger
- ½ teaspoon mace
- 1 tablespoon salt
- 4 cups sweet cider
- ½ cup molasses
- 2 lemons juiced and rind grated
- 2 oranges juiced and rind grated

Preheat oven to 425°. Pare, core and chop apples. Combine with all other ingredients and simmer 30 minutes or until flavors are blended. When baking pies, any fruit juice or a little wine may be added to moisten. Allow 3 cups for a 9 inch pie. Use a standard recipe for a two crust pie.

Fredith Shaw

Note

This recipe is usually prepared ahead of time and freezes very well. It can be thawed and used when convenient.

The Best Method of Preserving Apples

Put them into dry sand as soon as picked. It should be dried in the heat of summer and late in October put down the apples in layers with a covering of sand upon each layer.

Peachy Parker's Cookbook

Southern Squash Pie

Makes One Nine Inch Pie

A delightful alternative to pumpkin pie.

TO MAKE THE CRUST

Mix crust ingredients well and press firmly into buttered 9 inch pie pan. Chill crust until set, about 45 minutes.

TO MAKE THE PIE

Thaw squash to room temperature. Mix all other ingredients with hand beater or whisk for 2-3 minutes. Mix ingredients with squash over low heat, stirring constantly until mixture becomes very thick. Pour ingredients into pie crust and refrigerate overnight. Garnish with whipped cream.

June Slep

Note

Fresh squash may be used in place of the frozen squash.

For the Crust

- 18 graham crackers, crushed or 1½ cups crumbs
- ¼ cup sugar
- ½ cup melted butter or margarine

For the Pie

- 1 12-ounce box of frozen yellow squash
- 1 egg
- 1 tablespoon butter or margarine
- 1 tablespoon cornstarch
- 1 tablespoon vanilla
- ½ cup sugar
- 1 teaspoon cinnamon
- 1 teaspoon ginger
- 1 teaspoon nutmeg
- ½ can evaporated milk

Cure/Remedy for Overweight

Try this to reduce your weight. Get from a druggist 4 ounces of parnotis and dissolve it in a pint of hot water. Take a teaspoon of this harmless flesh reducer before each meal.

Nellie Cornman

DESSERTS

THE SOCIETY TODAY

The Cumberland County Historical Society and Hamilton Library Association is a non-profit organization dedicated to documenting the history and preserving the artifacts related to Cumberland County. Founded in 1874, the Cumberland County Historical Society is one of the oldest historical societies in the United States. The Society maintains a library, a museum and the Todd Lecture Hall in Carlisle, the county seat, and the recently bequeathed Two Mile House, a Federal stone farm house on five acres of land in South Middleton Township.

The library, begun with a bequest by John Hamilton and the donation of a few books, has grown into an important research facility. Included in the collection are books, manuscripts and monographs detailing the people and events which shaped Cumberland County from its earliest days. Unique among the library's collection are 30,000 photographs and 10,000 postcards which depict a wide spectrum of Cumberland County life and history.

The museum has gained its reputation by the rarity and significance of some of the objects in the collection. In addition to tools, clocks, furniture, textiles, paintings, ceramics and wood carvings, all of which were crafted in Cumberland County, the museum also includes several important and unique artifacts. Visitors to the museum may see among other things: a chair which belonged to James Wilson, a signer of the Declaration of Independence and an architect of the United States Constitution; the Goodman printing press, appraised by the Smithsonian Institution as the earliest of its kind known to exist in the country; noteworthy wood carvings by Wilhelm Schimmel and Aaron Mountz; and the Indian School Collection. The museum also features special exhibitions and lectures focusing on topics related to the history of Cumberland County.

In addition, the Society's publication program has been a hallmark of the Society since 1901. Its award winning journal is published semi annually. A renewed commitment to the production of professional quality books has resulted in the recent publication of five books. Featured topics include an architectural survey of county buildings, covered bridges, the Indian Industrial School, taverns of Cumberland County, and cloth and costume. This cookbook is the sixth publication in the Heritage series.

Education and programming complete the Society's mission by providing services to residents and visitors. Within the community, the Society provides an educational partnership with the County school system, lectures, tours, trips, historic house tours, the Landscape and Garden Forum and the award-winning Antiques Forum. Annually, 25,000 guests take advantage of the museum and library's resources. They travel from across the United States and internationally seeking general and specific information.

The Cumberland County Historical Society, dedicated to recording the past, is now looking to the future. In the year 2000, Cumberland County will celebrate the two hundred and fifieth anniversary of its founding. Presently the Society is embarking on an extensive building project. With its enthusiastic staff, dedicated volunteers and supportive patrons, the Society is looking forward to tackling the challenges of a new century of history for Cumberland County.

M.P.W.

CUMBERLAND COUNTY HISTORICAL SOCIETY

1996 BOARD OF DIRECTORS

ANDREA SHEYA, PRESIDENT

PAUL STRICKLER, VICE PRESIDENT

TITA EBERLY, SECRETARY

DAVID MacIVOR, TREASURER

KAREN BEST

TOM BIETSCH

JAMES D. FLOWER

ANN KRAMER HOFFER

JON F. LaFAVER

EDWARD K. MASLAND

ART McCARTER

GEORGE F. MYERS

FRED OYLER

ROBIN ROWE

WELLS SHOEMAKER

DIRECTORS EMERITI

JONAS WARRELL*

MILTON E. FLOWER*

PIERSON K. MILLER

WARREN GATES*

*deceased

CREDITS AND ACKNOWLEDGEMENTS

SUSAN D'LAMATER, *Design*

LINDA WITMER, EXECUTIVE DIRECTOR, CCHS
RICHARD TRITT, PHOTO CURATOR, CCHS
CCHS STAFF

MECHANICSBURG MUSEUM ASSOCIATION
SHIPPENSBURG HISTORICAL SOCIETY

JENNIFER GOLDSBOROUGH
OLIVER HAZAN
SUSAN JUMPER
CHARLES E. MACLAY
JEAN SOREM
CHARLES WENTZEL
BARBARA HOUSTON, *Proof Reader*

Recipe Testers
BEV BAKER
MARJORIE DUTREY
SONDRA ELIAS
MOLLY GARMAN
ROSALIE GEORGE
OLIVER HAZAN
ANN KRAMER HOFFER
GRETCHEN HOFFMAN
SUSAN JUMPER
VIRGINIA LaFOND
JACKIE MARTIN
CONNIE MIDDLETON
PATTI OWEN
ANNE PASS
MARY PERCIVAL
PAULA PRICE
MAUREEN REED
JEN STETTLER
ANDREA SHEYA
PAT STRICKLER
EILEEN SWIDLER
VIRGINIA WENTZEL
MARY PAT WENTZEL

CONTRIBUTORS

Peggy Adams · Marcie Addams · Patty Armbrust · Hilda Arnold · Helen Ashway · Marilyn Aust · Lois Barrick · Cathy Belcher · Karen Diener Best · Ruth Bietsch · George Kenneth Bishop · Maria Bishop · Judy Gallo Black · Ann Morris Blumenthal · Joan F. Bobb · Caroline Bogar · Virginia Bowden · Jeanne Bowers · Jill Bream · Louise Broujos · Margaret Bushey · Gail G. Callanan · Judy Castrina · Susan Cavenagh · Mary Caverly · Betty Chamberlin · Mary Jane Cooper · Ruth Coulson · Donna Cummings · Sylvia Dallas · Sandra Davis · Chris Deardorff · Frances Decker · Eleanor Deibert · Frances Del Duca · Maxim Dem'Chak · Mary Katherine Dennin · Ruth Diffenderfer · Maurita B. Diller · Freda Dillman · Bernadette Dineen · Susan Dossett · Marjorie Dutrey · Tita Eberly · Virginia Fickel Ehr · Damien Elias · Sondra Wolfe Elias · Mildred Ellerman · Sue Erdman · Elaine Faller · Carol Ferenz · Gladys Fields · Mary Filbert · Mary Finigan · Jane Fleisher · Doris Fowler · Doris Fraker · Frances Freet · Susan Fritschler · Marianne Fry · Ruth Fulton · Wendy Weary Gambini · Juan Garcia-Tuñon · Susan Garcia-Tuñon · Denise Garman · Molly Garman · Nancy George · Rosalie George · Hubert X. Gilroy · Sandra Gobrecht · Harry Golby · Ginnie Goodyear · Sandy Gority · Carol Green · Susan Green · Marguerite E. Grove · Gertrude Guise · Judy Hall · Shirley Halliday · Greg Harder · Jan Hays · Sally Haywood · Oliver Hazan · Isabelle Hazlett · Lydia Hazlett · Ruth Heberlig · Martha Heberleigh · Jane Heinze · Mary Snyder Hertzler · Freddie Highlands · Shelia Highlands · Mary Hock · Janet Hocker · Ann Kramer Hoffer · George Hoffer · Gretchen Hoffman · Sandra Hukill · Lorraine Humer · Linda Mohler Humes · Ann Hays Jacobs · Robert Lee Jacobs · Elizabeth Flower James · Bessie J. Jamieson · Florence Jay · Susan Jumper · Joan Jurgensen · Edna Kadel · Roxanne Kain · Marjorie Katzman · Debi Keith · Geoff Keith · Mary Kennedy · Ann King · Mary Wheeler King · Heather Kramer · Mary Kramer · Minnie Kramer · Connie Krout · Katy Krupp · Tammy Kutz · Virginia A. LaFond · Barbara Landis · Donna Landis · Lois Landis · Caren LaRue · Patricia Lehman · Vivian Leidy · Jane Lerch · Barbara Barnitz Lillich · Hwa Sun Loh · Joe Luciano · Lorraine Luciano · Margaret E. MacGregor · Charles E. Maclay · Nick Mallios · Roberta March · Market Cross Pub · Sara Crawley Marshall · Jackie Martin · Martha Martin · Edward Mashas · Debbie Masland · Elizabeth Masland · Sarah Haddock Masland · Barbara A. McCarthy · Elizabeth McCarthy · Robert McCarthy · Barbara McClain · Leana McCoy · Harriet McCrea · Susan McCrea · Pam Merlie · Glenn Miller, Sr. · Margaret Steck Miller · Elizabeth Minnich · Marjorie Mohler · Marjorie Mowery · Blanche W. Myers · Joyce Nelson · Trish Niemitz · Kathy Noaker · North Middleton Township Fire Co. · Mae Noss · Carolyn Craig Osborn · Patti Owen · Joanne Painter · Margaret W. L. Parker · Betty Parsell · Karen Pascuillo · Anne Pass · Wendell Pass · Mary Percival · Suzanne Phillippe · Helena B. Pickering · Marie Pinto · Jean Morris Portmann · Wilma B. Prescott · Paula Price · Salvatore Purpura · Jill Rahal · Pauline Raiser-Kee · Carol B. Reed · Laura Reed · Mary Thomas Reed · Maureen Reed · Sue Horner Reed · M. Susan Richman · Evelyn Rickert · Joe Rillo · Jean Ritter · Ann Harris Roeder · Ned Rosenbaum · Elizabeth Rousek · Janet Rutz · Wayne Rutz · Jean L. Saam · George M. Saegmuller · Hermione Saegmuller · Licia Sandberg · Mary Jane Sausser · Gladys Sawyer · Merri Lou Schaumann · Rita Schlansky · Dolly Scholl · Thora Schroeder · Virginia Schweiter · Catherine T. Scott · Lorraine Secrist · Dorothy Sehringer · Fredith Shaw · Andrea Sheya · James P. Sheya · Sara Shoemaker · Mary Louise Shuman · Pat Simms · June Slep · Betty Smith · Lyn Smith · Karen Sosbe · Susan Starr · Helen Stevens · Elizabeth Hean Stone · Olivia Straub · Pat Strickler · Emmy Robbins Stuart · Mary Wood Stuart · Betty Sullivan · Janet Surick · Eileen Swidler · Inez Taylor · Wesley R. Thompson · Betty Thrush · Holly Tiley · Zell Todd · Mabel Torrence · Amy Towne · Doris Townsend · Rosie Tregl · Ruth Tregl · June Trinnaman · Richard Tritt · Betty Wade · Dena Shadeck Walker · Marilyn Warrell · William Washington · Susan Watchorn · Betty Cornman Weary · Katie Weaver · Rev. Frederick S. Weiser · Arlene Wentzel · Chuck Wentzel · Mary Pat Wentzel · Virginia Wentzel · Deborah K. Westbrook · Ethel Wickard · Eve Wilkie · Jennifer Wilkie · Bea Williams · Rosa Willimeck · Nancy Wilson · Jack W. Wise · David Witmer · Linda F. Witmer · Peggy Wolf · Robert Wolf · Dot Wolfe · Gwen Wood · Marianna Wood · Anita Zimmerman

INDEX

1-2-3 Dressing for Pepper Slaw, p 101
18th Century Tavern Mint Punch, p 40

A Delicious Salad Dressing, p 100
A Gooey Shoo Fly Pie, p 283
Accompaniments, pp 189-197
    Apple Butter, p 197
    Brandied Peaches for Ham, p 189
    Grape Jam, p 195
    Homemade Mayonnaise, p 191
    Hot Mustard, p 191
    Lemon Butter, p 195
    Manitoba Pickles, p 192
    Marvelous Marmalade, p 194
    Rhubarb Chutney, p 189
    Rhubarb Pineapple Compote, p 190
    Sunny Strawberry Preserves, p 194
Aegean Chicken Breasts, p 139
Almonds
    Almond Cheese Strips, p 16
    Chocolate Almond Crunch, p 263
    English Butter Toffee, p 261
    Nut Meringue Slices, p 259
Amaretto Chicken, p135
Amazing Cracker Chunks, p 254
Anise Bread, p 218
Antoinette's Sherry Punch, p 42
Apple
    Apple Butter, p 197
    Apple-Orange Sweet Potato Galette, p 174
    Baked Apple Alaska, p 266
    Cinnamon Apples, p 267
    Deluxe Apple Pie, p 274
    Dilled Apple-Chicken Salad, p 73
    Pear and Apple Compote, p 207
    Tart Tatin, p 273
Apple Sauce
    Applesauce Cake, p 236
    Gram's Apple Surprise, p 265
    Jonathan's Favorite Cake, p 242
Arroz Con Pollo, p 136
Arugula
    Mushroom & Arugula Risotto, p 177
Asparagus
    Asparagus Supreme, p 158
    Stir-Fried Asparagus with Cashews, p 159
Aunt Christine's Breakfast Cake, p 209
Aunt Kate's Meatballs, p 118
Aunt Katherine's Pound Cake, p 241
Aunt Pearl's Lemon Cheese Icing, p 241
Aunt Ruth's Lemon Sponge Pie, p 277

Bacon
    Almond Cheese Strips, p 16
    Breakfast Squares, p 208
    Broccoli Salad, p 81
    Lowensahn (dandelion) Salad, p 84
    Old Fashioned Wilted Lettuce, p 97
    Scrambled Eggs Pie, p 202
    Spinach Filled Tomatoes, p 178
    Spinach Salad, p 89
    Wilted Greens with Sweet and Sour Sauce, p 97
    Zucchini Salad with Hot Bacon Dressing, p 95
Baked Apple Alaska, p 266
Baked Beans, p 159
Baked Cheese Dip, p 16
Baked Chicken Fantastic, p 129

Baked Corn on the Cob, p 164
Baked Rice Pudding, p 268
Baked Seafood Supreme, p 143
Bar-B- Q Meatballs, p 33
Beans
    Baked Beans, p 159
    Black Bean Hummus, p 32
    Black Bean Ole, p 32
    Black Bean Salad, p 78
    Crumbly Green Beans, p 169
    Sweet Pickle Bean Salad, p 79
    Vegetarian Chili, p 63
    White Chili, p 64
Beef   106-111,121,122
    Aunt Kate's Meatballs, p 118
    Bar-B-Q Meatballs, p 33
    Chocolate Shop Sandwich Filling, p 35
    Coney Island Hot Dog Sauce, p 185
    Corned Beef and Vegetable Medley, p 107
    East Steak Diane, p 110
    English Cottage Pie, p 122
    Filet Mignon Superb, p 109
    Filet of Beef with Sour Cream, p 106
    Grilled Flank Steak, p 111
    Hot Pecan Pie, p 16
    Hunter's Stew, p 125
    Lobster Stuffed Tenderloin, p 108
    Mince Meat Pie, p 284
    Worldly Beef Stroganoff, p 121
Beer Bread, p 219
Beets
    Chinese Pickled Beets, p 160
Beverages, pp 40-47
    18th Century Tavern Mint Punch, p 40
    Antoinette's Sherry Punch, p 42
    Bloody Mary, p 47
    Egg Nog, p 44
    Grandma's Mint Julep, p 44
    Mrs Bosler's Champagne Punch, p 42
    Party Punch, p 40
    Pink Ladies, p 45
    Tea Punch, p 46
    Wassail, p 45
    Your Own Wine, p 46
Bill Washington's Chicken Souffle, p 132
Black and White Bread Pudding, p 269
Black Bean Hummus, p 32
Black Bean Ole, p 32
Black Bean Salad, p 78
Bloody Mary, p 47
Blue Cheese Dressing, p 103
Braised Lamb Stew, p 124
Brandied Peaches for Country Ham, p 189
Breads, pp 218-233
    Anise Bread, p 218
    Beer Bread, p 219
    Dill Bread, p 220
    Family Rolls, p 226
    Focaccia, p 223
    French Bread, p 224
    French Rolls, p 227
    Healthy Muffins, p 228
    Honey Wheat Bread, p 229
    Hot Cheddar Cheese Bread, p 220
    Onion Cheese Bread, p 221
    Pizza Dough, p 230

Polish Easter Bread, p 231
Raisin Gems, p 233
Raisin Pumpernickel Bread, p 232
Vienna Bread, p 233, p 218-233

Breakfast, pp 200-215
Aunt Christine's Breakfast Cake, p 209
Breakfast Squares, p 208
Broccoli Ham Rollups, p 200
Brunch Bake, p 201
Cinnamon Twists, p 213
Cream Scones, p 210
Crumb Pies, p 209
Egg Omelette for Twelve, p 203
Egg Souffle, p 203
Fritatta, p 204
Pear and Apple Compote, p 207
Pennsylvania Fresh Corn Fritters, p 208
Popover Pie, p 206
Raspberry Sauce, p 206
Scrambled Eggs Pie, p 202
Sour Cream Coffeecake, p 210
Sticky Buns, p 211
Uncle Annie's Famous Pancakes, p 214
Versatile Cheese Strata, p 205
Waffles, p 215
Whole Wheat Pancakes, p 214

Broccoli
Broccoli Ham Rollups, p 200
Broccoli Salad, p 81
Broccoli, Snow Pea & Baby Corn Salad, p 80
Chicken and Broccoli, p 128
Greens with Garlic, Raisins & Pine Nuts, p 168
Spicy Sweet Broccoli, p 161

Brunch Bake, p 201

Brussels Sprouts
Marinated Brussels Sprouts, p 36

Butter Crunch Squares, p 256
Butterflied Leg of Lamb, p 123
Buttermilk Coconut Custard Pie, p 278

Cabbage
1-2-3 Dressing for Pepper Slaw, p 101
Cabbage and Kielbasa Soup, p 58
Crunchy Spinach Cabbage Salad, p 90
Corned Beef and Vegetable Medley, p 107
Halushki, p 161
Hog Maw, p 114
Low Cal Vegetable Slaw, p 93
No-Mayo Cole Slaw, p 93
Perfection Salad, p 98

Cakes, p 236-248
Applesauce Cake, p 236
Aunt Katherine's Pound Cake, p 241
Aunt Pearl's Lemon Cheese Icing, p 241
Carrot Cake, p 238
Centerpiece Coconut Cake, p 239
Date Nut Cake, p 242
Gingerbread, p 248
Italian Creme Cake, p 245
Jimmy Carter Cake, p 237
Jonathan's Favorite Cake, p 242
Karithopeta, p 244
Shoo Fly Cupcakes, p 236
Sir Hubert's Irish Whiskey Cake, p 243
Velvet Cheese Cake, p 247
White Chocolate Fudge Cake, p 246

Candy, pp 261-264
Chocolate Almond Crunch, p 263
English Butter Toffee, p 261
No Fail Fudge, p 264
Peanut Butter Easter Eggs, p 263

Carrots
Cardamom Carrots, p 162
Carrot Cake, p 238
Carrot Souffle, p 162
Ginger Carrots, p 163

Cashew(s)
Cashew Chicken, p 126
Stir-Fried Asparagus with Cashews, p 159

Caviar Cheesecake, p 20
Celebration Shrimp Salad, p 77

Celery Root
Gratin of Celery Root and Potato, p 163

Centerpiece Coconut Cake, p 239

Chard
Wilted Greens with Sweet and Sour Sauce, p 97

Cheese
Almond Cheese Strips, p 16
Baked Cheese Dip, p 17
Caviar Cheesecake, p 20
Chicken Parmesan, p 131
Chocolate Shop Sandwich Filling, p 35
Cocktail Cheese Sandwiches, p 35
Golden Parmesan Potatoes, p 171
Hot Cheddar Cheese Bread, p 220
Special Cheese Spread, p 20
Versatile Cheese Strata, p 205

Cheesecake
Caviar Cheesecake, p 20
Velvet Cheesecake, p247

Chicken, p 126-141
Aegean Chicken Breasts, p 139
Amaretto Chicken, p 135
Arroz Con Pollo, p 136
Baked Chicken Fantastic, p 129
Bill Washington's Chicken Souffle, p 132
Cashew Chicken, p 126
Chicken and Broccoli, p 128
Chicken Canapes, p 24
Chicken Casablanca, p 138
Chicken Corn Noodle Soup, p 51
Chicken Corn Soup, p 51
Chicken Lasagna, p 133
Chicken Parmesan, p 131
Chicken Satay, p 27
Chicken Tunon, p 137
Chicken with Sausage and Mushrooms, p 128
Cumberland Chicken Salad, p 72
Curried Chicken Beasts, p 127
Dad's Austrian Goulash, p 120
Dilled Apple-Chicken Salad, p 73
Fancy Chicken Pot Pie, p 141
Fruited Chicken and Rice Salad, p 74
Hot Chicken Salad, p 75
Liver Pate, p 30
Mexican Chicken Kiev, p 131
Orange Honey Mustard Chicken, p 130
Regal Chicken Salad, p 76
The Best Meatballs, p 119
Two Mile Chicken, p 129
White Chili, p 64

Chili

Vegetarian Chili, p 63
White Chili, p 64
Chinese Pickled Beets, p 160
Chioppino, p 52
Chocolate Almond Crunch, p 263
Chocolate Shop Sandwich Filling, p 35
Cinnamon Apples, p 267
Cinnamon Twists, p 213
Clams
 Linguine with White Clam Sauce, p 150
 Zuppa Di Pesce, p 151
Cocktail Cheese Sandwich, p 35
Coconut
 Buttermilk Coconut Custard Pie, p 278
 Centerpiece Coconut Cake, p 239
Coney Island Hot Dog Sauce, p 185
Cookies, p 249-260
 Amazing Cracker Chunks, p 254
 Banana Gingers, p 249
 Butter Crunch Squares, p 256
 Divine Dessert Bars, p 258
 Double Quick Date Dessert, p 254
 Drop Sand Tarts, p 250
 Filled Cookies, p 253
 Fudgelicious Brownies, p 260
 Gobs, p 255
 Grandma Harris' Frosted Chewies, p 256
 Grandma Shadeck's Ice Box cookies, p 257
 Martha Washington Ginger Cookies, p 249
 Moravian Ginger Cookies, p 250
 Nut Meringue Slices, p 259
 Sand Tarts, p 251
Corn
 Baked Corn on the Cob, p 164
 Broccoli, Snow Peas and Baby Corn Salad, p 80
 Chicken Corn Noodle Soup, p 51
 Chicken Corn Soup, p 51
 Corn Pie, p 165
 Corn Pudding, p 165
 Creamed Corn Soup, p 50
 Pennsylvania Fresh Corn Fritters, p 208
Corned Beef and Vegetable Medley, p 107
Couscous
 Fruited Couscous Salad, p 82
 Vegetable Couscous, p 174
Crab
 Baked Seafood Supreme, p 143
 Chioppino, p 52
 Crab Cakes, p 143
 Crab Dip, p 22
 Crab Maryland, p 142
 Crab Meat Bisque, p 53
 Molded Crab Spread, p 22
 New Orleans Crab Salad, p 77
 She-Crab Soup, p 53
 Versatile Cheese Strata, p 205
Cranberry
 Cranberry Sauce, p 184
 Fruited Chicken and Rice Salad, p 74
 Holiday Salad, p 99
Cream of Potato Soup, p 67
Cream Pie, p 276
Cream Scones, p 210
Creamed Corn Soup, p 50
Crostini Caponata, p 36
Crumb Pies, p 209

Crumbly Green Beans, p 169
Crunchy Spinach Cabbage Salad, p 90
Cucumber
 Cucumber Sandwiches, p 34
 Grilled Salmon with Cucumber-Yogurt Sauce, p 144
 Iced Cucumber Soup, p 68
 Low Cal Dip, p 25
 Manitoba Pickles, p 192
 Summer Cucumbers and Onions, p 94
Cumberland Chicken Salad, p 72
Cumberland Creek Tartare Sauce, p 184
Curried Chicken Breasts, p 127

Dad's Austrian Goulash, p 120
Date
 Date Nut Cake, p 242
 Double Quick Date Dessert, p 254
Deluxe Apple Pie, p 274
Desserts, pp 234-285
 A Gooey Shoo Fly Pie, p 283
 Amazing Cracker Chunks, p 254
 Applesauce Cake, p 236
 Aunt Katherine's Pound Cake, p 241
 Aunt Pearl's Lemon Cheese Icing, p 241
 Aunt Ruth's Lemon Sponge Pie, p 277
 Baked Apple Alaska, p 266
 Baked Rice Pudding, p 268
 Banana Gingers, p 249
 Black and White Bread Pudding, p 269
 Butter Crunch Squares, p 256
 Buttermilk Coconut Custard Pie, p 278
 Carrot Cake, p 238
 Centerpiece Coconut Cake, p 239
 Chocolate Almond Crunch, p 263
 Cinnamon Apples, p 267
 Date Nut Cake, p 242
 Deluxe Apple Pie, p 274
 Divine Dessert Bars, p 258
 Double Quick Date Dessert, p 254
 Drop Sand Tarts, p 250
 English Butter Toffee, p 261
 Filled Cookies, p 253
 Fresh Peach Meringue Pie, p 279
 Fruit Cream Pie, p 276
 Fudgelicious Brownies, p 260
 Gingerbread, p 248
 Gobs, p 255
 Graham Cracker Roll, p 265
 Gram's Apple Surprise, p 265
 Grandma Harris' Frosted Chewies, p 256
 Grandma Shadeck's Ice Box Cookies, p 257
 Grandmother's Black Raspberry Pie, p 275
 Grapefruit Pie, p 277
 Homestead Raisin Pie, p 280
 Italian Creme Cake, p 245
 Jimmy Carter Cake, p 237
 Jonathan's Favorite Cake, p 242
 Kahlua Pecan Pie, p 282
 Karithopeta, p 244
 Lemon Sponge Pudding, p 268
 Martha Washington Ginger Cookies, p 249
 Mince Meat Pie, p 284
 Moravian Ginger Cookies, p 250
 No Fail Fudge, p 264
 Nut Meringue Slices, p 259
 Peanut Butter Easter Eggs, p 263

        Pecan Pumpkin Pie, p 282
        Raspberry-Brownie Ice Cream Cake, p 272
        Rhubarb Tapioca Pudding, p 270
        Sand Tarts, p 251
        Shoo Fly Cupcakes, p 236
        Sir Hubert's Irish Whiskey Cake, p 243
        Southern Squash Pie, p 285
        Spanish Cream, p 270
        Sweet Potato Pie, p 281
        Tart Tatin, p 273
        Velvet Cheese Cake, p 247
        White Chocolate Fudge Cake, p 246
Dill Bread, p 220
Dilled Apple-chicken Salad, p 73
Divine Dessert Bars, p 258
Double Quick Date Dessert, p 254
Drop Sand Tarts, p 250
Dutch Sweet and Sour Dressing, p 100

Easy Steak Diane, p 110
Egg
        Aunt Christine's Breakfast Cake, p 209
        Breakfast Squares, p 208
        Brunch Bake, p 201
        Egg Nog, p 44
        Egg Omelette for Twelve, p 203
        Egg Souffle, p 203
        Fritatta, p 204
        Scrambled Eggs Pie, p 202
        Versatile Cheese Strata, p 205
Eggplant
        Ratatouille, p 170
Endive Watercress and Pomegranate Salad, p 92
English Butter Toffee, p 261
English Cottage Pie, p 122
Entrees, pp 106-155
        Aegean Chicken Breasts, p 139
        Amaretto Chicken, p 135
        Arroz Con Pollo, p 136
        Aunt Kate's Meatballs, p 118
        Baked Chicken Fantastic, p 129
        Baked Seafood Supreme, p 143
        Bill Washington's Chicken Souffle, p 132
        Braised Lamb Stew, p 124
        Butterflied Leg of Lamb, p 123
        Cashew Chicken, p 126
        Chicken and Broccoli, p 128
        Chicken Casablanca, p 138
        Chicken Lasagna, p 133
        Chicken Parmesan, p 131
        Chicken Tunon, p 137
        Chicken with Sausage and Mushrooms, p 128
        Corned Beef and Vegetable Medley, p 107
        Crab Cakes, p 143
        Crab Maryland, p 142
        Curried Chicken Breasts, p 127
        Dad's Austrian Goulash, p 120
        East Steak Diane, p 110
        English Cottage Pie, p 122
        Fancy Chicken Pot Pie, p 141
        Filet Mignon Superb, p 109
        Filet of Beef with Sour Cream, p 106
        Grandma G's Ham Barbecue, p 114
        Grilled Flank Steak, p 111
        Grilled Pork Chops with Salad, p 116
        Grilled Salmon with Cucumber-Yogurt Sauce, p 144
        Grilled Salmon with Watercress, p 145
        Heavenly Fish Fillets, p 151
        Hog Maw, p 114
        Hunter's Stew, p 125
        Lamb Medallions, p 123
        Linguine with White Clam Sauce, p 150
        Lisburn Lasagna, p 153
        Lobster Stuffed Tenderloin, p 108
        Mexican Chicken Kiev, p 131
        Orange Honey Mustard Chicken, p 130
        Peach Glazed Spareribs, p 115
        Penne with Red Pepper Sauce, p 154
        Poached Salmon, p 147
        Pork Tenderloin with Orange Sauce, p 117
        Salmon Monte Carlo, p 145
        Shrimp de Jonghe, p 148
        Shrimp Mediterranean, p 146
        Shrimp Pilaf, p 149
        Skillet Pork Chops, p 117
        Sour Cream Enchiladas, p 155
        Stromboli, p 152
        Sweet Ham and Pork, p 115
        The Best Meatballs, p 119
        Two Mile Chicken, p 129
        Veal Cutlets with Spinach, p 112
        Veal Marsala, p 113
        Worldly Beef Stroganoff, p 121
        Zuppa Di Pesce, p 151

Family Rolls, p 226
Fancy Chicken Pot Pie, p 141
Filet Mignon Superb, p 109
Filet of Beef with Sour Cream, p 106
Filled Cookies, p 253
Fish
        Chioppino, p 52
        Heavenly Fish Fillets, p 151
Focaccia, p 223
French Bread, p 224
French Rolls, p 227
Fresh Peach Meringue Pie, p 279
Frittata, p 204
Fruit Cream Pie, p 276
Fruited Chicken and Rice Salad, p 74
Fruited Couscous, p 82
Fudgelious Brownies, p 260

Gelatin
        Perfection Salad, p 98
        Spanish Cream, p 270
German Potato Salad, p 88
Ginger Carrots, p 163
Gingerbread, p 248
Gobs, p 255
Golden Parmesan Potatoes, p 171
Graham Cracker Roll, p 265
Gram's Apple Surprise, p 265
Grandma G's Ham Barbeque, p 114
Grandma Harris' Frosted Chewies, p 256
Grandma Shadecks Ice Box Cookies, p 257
Grandma's Mint Juleps, p 44
Grandmother's Black Raspberry Pie, p 275
Grape Jam, p 195
Grapefruit Pie, p 277
Gratin of Celery Root and Potato, p 163
Greek Salad, p 82
Green Vegetable Dip, p 24

Greens with Garlic, Raisins and Pine Nuts, p 168
Grilled Flank Steak, p 111
Grilled Pork Chops with Salad, p 116
Grilled Salmon with Cucumber Yogurt Sauce, p 144
Grilled Salmon with Watercress, p 145

Halushki, p 161
Ham
    Broccoli Ham Rollups, p 200
    Grandma G's Ham Barbecue, p 114
    Stromboli, p 152
    Sweet Ham and Pork, p 115
Hamburger Soup, p 61
Hawaiian Sea Anemones, p 28
Healthy Muffins, p 228
Hean Oyster Sauce, p 187
Heavenly Fish Fillets, p 151
Hog Maw, p 114
Holiday Salad, p 99
Homemade Mayonnaise, p 191
Homestead Raisin Pie, p 280
Honey Wheat Bread, p 229
Hors D'Oeuvres, pp 14-39
    Almond Cheese Strips, p 16
    Baked Cheese Dip, p 17
    Bar-B-Q Meatballs, p 33
    Black Bean Ole, p 32
    Caviar Cheesecake, p 20
    Chicken Canapes, p 24
    Chicken Satay, p 27
    Chocolate Shop Sandwich Filling, p 35
    Cocktail Cheese Sandwiches, p 35
    Crab Dip, p 22
    Crostini Caponata, p 36
    Cucumber Sandwiches, p 34
    Green Vegetable Dip, p 24
    Hawaiian Sea Anemones, p 28
    Hot Pecan Pie, p 17
    Liver Pate, p 30
    Low Cal Dip, p 25
    Marinated Brussels Sprouts, p 36
    Minted Melon Balls, p 37
    Molded Crab Spread, p 22
    Monte Carlo Spread, p 17
    Mushroom Pate, p 38
    Nacho Mushrooms, p 38
    Olive Nut Spread, p 18
    Peanut Sauce, p 27
    Pecan Cheese Log, p 19
    Pesto & Sun Dried Tomato Torte, p 21
    Special Cheese Spread, p 20
    Sweet Spicy Pecans, p 39
    Watercress Sandwiches, p 34
Hot Cheddar Cheese Bread, p 220
Hot Chicken Salad, p 75
Hot Mustard, p 191
Hot Pecan Pie, p 17
Hunter's Stew, p 125

Iced Cucumber Soup, p 68
Icing, pp 238, 239, 244, 245, 255, 258, 260
Indian Rice, p 175
Italian Creme Cake, p 245
Italian Sausage Soup, p 60
Italian Vegetable and Pasta Toss, p 85

Jimmy Carter Cake, p 237

Jonathan's Favorite Cake, p 242
Julienne Vegetable Saute, p 180

Kahula Pecan Pie, p 282
Karithopeta, p 244
Kielbasa
    Cabbage and Kielbasa Soup, p 58

Lamb, pp 123, 124
    Braised Lamb Stew, p 124
    Butterflied Leg of Lamb, p 123
    Lamb Medallions, p 123
    The Best Meatballs, p 119
Lasagna
    Chicken Lasagna, p 133
    Lisburn Lasagna, p 153
Lemon
    Aunt Pearl's Lemon Cheese Icing, p 241
    Aunt Ruth's Lemon Sponge Pie, p 277
    Lemon Butter, p 195
    Lemon Sponge Pudding, p 268
Linguine with White Clam Sauce, p 150
Lisburn Lasagna, p 153
Liver Pate, p 30
Lobster
    Chioppino, p 52
    Lobster Stuffed Tenderloin, p 108
Low Cal Dip, p 25
Low Cal Vegetable Slaw, p 93
Lowensahn (Dandelion) Salad, p 84

Main Line Mashed Potatoes, p 171
Manitoba Pickles, p 192
Marinated Brussels Sprouts, p 36
Martha Washington Ginger Cookies, p 249
Marvelous Marmalade, p 194
Mexican Chicken Kiev, p 131
Mince Meat Pie, p 284
Minted Melon Balls, p 37
Molded Crab Spread, p 22
Monte Carlo Spread, p 17
Moore Hash Browns, p 173
Moravian Ginger Cookies, p 250
Mrs. Bosler's Champagne Punch, p 42
Mushroom and Arugula Risotto, p 177
Mushroom
    Chicken with Sausage and Mushrooms, p 128
    Mushroom & Arugula Risotto, p 177
    Mushroom Pate, p 38
    Mushroom Vegetable Soup, p 65
    Nacho Mushrooms, p 38

Nacho Mushrooms, p 38
New Orleans Crab Salad, p 77
No Fail Fudge, p 264
No Mayo Cole Slaw, p 93
Nut Meringue Slices, p 259

Oatmeal Soup, p 66
Old Fashioned Cooked Salad Dressing, p 101
Old Fashioned Wilted Lettuce, p 97
Olive Nut Spread, p 18
Onion Cheese Bread, p 221
Orange
    Apple-Orange Sweet Potato Galette, p 174
    Marvelous Marmalade, p 194
    Orange Cream Fruit Salad, p 99

Orange Honey Mustard Chicken, p 130
Orange Salad Dressing, p 102
Orzo Salad, p 87
Oysters
    Hean Oyster Sauce, p 187
    Oyster Sauce for Ham, p 186
    Oyster Stewpendous, p 54

Pancakes
    Uncle Annie's Famous Pancakes, p214
    Whole Wheat Pancakes, p 214
Party Punch, p 40
Pasta
    Chicken Lasagna, p 133
    Italian Sausage Soup, p 60
    Lisburn Lasagna, p 153
    New Orleans Crab Salad, p 77
    Penne with Red Pepper Sauce, p 154
    Salmon Monte Carlo, p 145
    Zuppa Di Pesce, p 151
Pat's Potato Salad, p 88
Peach
    Brandied Peaches for Ham, p 189
    Fresh Peach Meringue Pie, p 279
    Orange Cream Fruit Salad, p 99
    Peach Glazed Spareribs, p 115
Peanut Butter Easter Eggs, p 263
Peanut Sauce, p 27
Pear and Apple Compote, p 207
Peas
    Broccoli, Snow Pea & Baby Corn Salad, p 80
    Potage Saint-Cloud, p 67
Pecan
    Hot Pecan Pie, p 17
    Kahula Pecan Pie, p 282
    Pecan Cheese Log, p 19
    Pecan Pumpkin Pie, p 282
    Pumpkin Pecan Soup, p 66
    Sweet Spicy Pecans, p 39
Penne with Red Pepper Sauce, p 154
Pennsylvania Fresh Corn Fritters, p 208
Peppers, Red
    Penne with Red Pepper Sauce, p 154
Perfection Salad, p 98
Pesto Sundried Tomato Torte, p 21
Pickles
    Manitoba Pickles, p 192
Pie Crust, pp 275, 276, 279, 285
Pies, pp 274-285
    A Gooey Shoo Fly Pie, p 283
    Aunt Ruth's Lemon Sponge Pie, p 277
    Buttermilk Coconut Custard Pie, p 278
    Cream Pie, p 277
    Deluxe Apple Pie, p 274
    Fresh Peach Meringue Pie, p 279
    Fruit Cream Pie, p 276
    Grandmother's Black Raspberry Pie, p 275
    Homestead Raisin Pie, p 280
    Kahula Pecan Pie, p 282
    Mince Meat Pie, p 284
    Pecan Pumpkin Pie, p 282
    Southern Squash Pie, p 285
    Sweet Potato Pie, p 281
Pineapple
    Rhubarb Pineapple Compote, p 190
Pink Ladies, p 45

Pizza Dough, p 230
Poached Salmon, p 147
Polish Easter Bread, p 231
Pomegranate
    Endive, Watercress & Pomegranate Salad, p 92
Popover Pie, p 206
Pork, pp 114-117
    Aunt Kate's Meatballs, p 118
    Dad's Austrian Goulash, p 120
    Grandma G's Ham Barbecue, p 114
    Grilled Pork Chops with Salad, p 116
    Hog Maw, p 114
    Hunter's Stew, p 125
    Peach Glazed Spareribs, p 115
    Pork Tenderloin with Orange Sauce, p 117
    Skillet Pork Chops, p 117
    Sweet Ham and Pork, p 115
Potage Saint-Cloud, p 67
Potato
    Cream of Potato Soup, p 67
    German Potato Salad, p 88
    Golden Parmesan Potatoes, p 171
    Gratin of Celery Root and Potato, p 163
    Hog Maw, p 114
    Main Line Mashed Potatoes, p 171
    Moore Hash Browns, p 173
    Pat's Potato Salad, p 88
    Potato Filling, p 172
    Skillet Pork Chops, p 117
Pumpernickel Bread
    Baked Cheese Dip, p 17
    Raisin Pumpernickel Bread, 232
Pumpkin Pecan Soup, p 66

Raisin
    Filled Cookies, p 253
    Raisin Gems, p 233
    Raisin Pumpernickel Bread, 232
    Raisin Sauce for Ham, p 186
Raspberry
    Grandmother's Black Raspberry Pie, p 275
    Raspberry-Brownie Ice Cream Cake, p 272
    Raspberry Sauce, p 206
Ratatouille, p 170
Regal Chicken Salad, p 76
Rhubarb
    Rhubarb Chutney, p 189
    Rhubarb Pineapple Compote, p 190
    Rhubarb Tapioca Pudding, p 270
Rice
    Arroz Con Pollo, p 136
    Baked Rice Pudding, p 268
    Fruited Chicken and Rice Salad, p 74
    Indian Rice, p 175
    Mushroom & Arugula Risotto, p 177
    Seasoned Onion Rice, p 175
    Shrimp Pilaf, p 149
    Wild Rice Salad, p 86

Salad Dressing, pp 100-103
    1-2-3 Dressing for Pepper Slaw, p 101
    A Delicious Salad Dressing, p 100
    Blue Cheese Dressing, p 103
    Dutch Sweet and Sour Dressing, p 100
    Old Fashioned Cooked Salad Dressing, p 101

Orange Salad Dressing, p 102
Salads, pp 72-103
    Black Bean Salad, p 78
    Broccoli, Salad, p 81
    Broccoli, Snow Pea & Baby Corn Salad, p 80
    Celebration Shrimp Salad, p 77
    Crunchy Spinach Cabbage Salad, p 90
    Cumberland Chicken Salad, p 72
    Dilled Apple-chicken Salad, p 73
    Endive, Watercress & Pomegranate Salad, p 92
    Fruited Chicken and Rice Salad, p 74
    Fruited Couscous Salad, p 82
    German Potato Salad, p 88
    Greek Salad, p 82
    Hot Chicken Salad, p 75
    Italian Vegetable & Pasta Toss, p 85
    Low Cal Vegetable Slaw, p 92
    Lowensahn (dandelion) Salad, p 84
    New Orleans Crab Salad, p 77
    No-Mayo Cole Slaw, p 93
    Old Fashioned Wilted Lettuce, p 97
    Orzo Salad, p 87
    Pat's Potato Salad, p 88
    Perfection Salad, p 98
    Regal Chicken Salad, p 76
    Simply Super Tomatoes, p 94
    Spinach Salad, p 89
    Spinach Waldorf Salad, p 89
    Splendid Strawberry Spinach Salad, p 91
    Stuffed Cymlins with a Flavored Vinaigrette, p 96
    Summer Cucumbers & Onions, p 94
    Sweet Pickle Bean Salad, p 79
    Wild Rice Salad, p 86
    Wilted Greens with Sweet and Sour Sauce, p 97
    Zucchini Salad with Hot Bacon Dressing, p 95
Salmon
    Grilled Salmon with Cucumber-Yogurt Sauce, p 144
    Grilled Salmon with Watercress, p 145
    Poached Salmon, p 147
    Salmon Monte Carlo, p 145
Sand Tarts, p 250, 251
Sandwiches
    Chocolate Shop Sandwich Filling, p 35
    Cocktail Cheese Sandwich, p 35
    Cucumber Sandwiches, p 34
    Grandma G's Ham Barbecue, p 114
    Stromboli, p 152
    Watercress Sandwich, p 34
Sauces
    Coney Island Hot Dog Sauce, p 185
    Cranberry Sauce, p 184
    Cumberland Creek Tartare Sauce, p 184
    Hean Oyster Sauce, p 187
    Oyster Sauce for Ham, p 186
    Raisin Sauce for Ham, p 186
    Sauce Indienne, p 185
    Spaghetti Sauce, p 188
Sausage
    Chicken with Sausage and Mushrooms, p 128
Savory Tomato Soup, p 69
Scallop Chowder, p 56
Scrambled Egg Pie, p 202
Seafood, pp 142-151
    Baked Seafood Supreme, p 143
    Crab Cakes, p 143
    Crab Maryland, p 142
    Grilled Salmon with Watercress, p 145
    Grilled Salmon with Cucumber-Yogurt Sauce, p 144
    Heavenly Fish Fillets, p 151
    Linguine with White Clam Sauce, p 150
    Poached Salmon, p 147
    Salmon Monte Carlo, p 145
    Shrimp de Jonghe, p 148
    Shrimp Mediterranean, p 146
    Shrimp Pilaf, p 149
    Zuppa Di Pesce, p 151
Seasoned Onion Rice, p 175
She Crab Soup, p 53
Shoo Fly Cupcakes, p 236
Shrimp
    Celebration Shrimp Salad, p 77
    Hawaiian Sea Anemones, p 28
    Shrimp De Jonghe, p 148
    Shrimp Mediterranean, p 146
    Shrimp Pilaf, p 149
    Zuppa Di Pesce, p 151
Simply Super Tomatoes, p 94
Skillet Pork Chops, p 117
Soups, pp 48-69
    Cabbage and Kielbasa Soup, p 58
    Chicken Corn Noodle Soup, p 51
    Chicken Corn Soup, p 51
    Chioppino, p 52
    Crab Meat Bisque, p 53
    Cream of Potato Soup, p 67
    Creamed Corn Soup, p 50
    Hamburger Soup, p 61
    Iced Cucumber Soup, p 68
    Italian Sausage Soup, p 60
    Mushroom Vegetable Soup, p 65
    Oatmeal Soup, p 66
    Oyster Stewpendous, p 54
    Potage Saint-Cloud, p 67
    Pumpkin Pecan Soup, p 66
    Savory Tomato Soup, p 69
    Scallop Chowder, p 56
    She-Crab Soup, p 53
    Strawberry Velvet Soup, p 69
    Tortellini Soup, p 62
    Tuna Cheese Chowder, p 57
    Vegetable Soup, p 59
    Vegetarian Chili, p 63
    White Chili, p 64
Sour Cream Coffee Cake, p 210
Sour Cream Enchiladas, p 155
Southern Squash Pie, p 285
Spaghetti Sauce, p 188
Spanish Cream, p 270
Special Cheese Spread, p 20
Spicy Sweet Broccoli, p 161
Spinach
    Crunchy Spinach Cabbage Salad, p 90
    Spinach Filled Tomatoes, p 178
    Spinach Salad, p 89
    Spinach Waldorf Salad, p 89
    Splendid Strawberry Spinach Salad, p 91
    Veal Cutlets with Spinach, p 112
    Wilted Greens with Sweet and Sour Sauce, p 97
Splendid Strawberry Spinach Salad, p 91
Squash
    Southern Squash Pie, p 285
    Summer Squash Supreme, p 178

St. Hubert's Irish Whiskey Cake, p 243
Sticky Buns, p 211
Stir Fried Asparagus, p 159
Strawberry
    Splendid Strawberry Spinach Salad, p 91
    Strawberry Velvet Soup, p 69
    Sunny Strawberry Preserves, p 194
Stromboli, p 152
Stuffed Cymlins with Flavored Vinaigrette, p 96
Summer Cucumbers and Onions, p 94
Summer Squash Supreme, p 178
Sunny Strawberry Preserves, p 194
Sweet Ham and Pork, p 115
Sweet Pickle Bean Salad, p 79
Sweet Potatoes
    Apple-Orange Sweet Potato Galette, p 174
    Sweet Potato Pie, p 281
Sweet Spicy Pecans, p 39

Tapioca
    Rhubarb Tapioca Pudding, p 270
Tart Tatin, p 273
Tea Punch, p 46
The Best Meatballs, p 119
Tomato
    Crostini Caponata, p 36
    Pesto & Sun Dried Tomato Torte, p 21
    Ratatouille, p 170
    Savory Tomato Soup, p 69
    Simply Super Tomatoes, p 94
    Spaghetti Sauce, p 188
    Spinach Filled Tomatoes, p 178
    Stuffed Cymlins with a Flavored Vinaigrette, p 96
    Tomato Pudding, p 179
    Tomatoes and Zucchini Oriental, p 179
Tortellini Soup, p 62
Tuna Cheese Chowder, p 57
Two Mile Chicken, p 129

Uncle Annie's Famous Pancakes, p 214

Veal, pp 112,113
    Aunt Kate's Meatballs, p 118
    Dad's Austrian Goulash, p 120
    The Best Meatballs, p 119
    Veal Cutlets with Spinach, p 112
    Veal Marsala, p 113
Vegetable Couscous, p 174
Vegetable Soup, p 59
Vegetables and Side Dishes, p 158-181
    Apple-Orange Sweet Potato Galette, p 174
    Asparagus Supreme, p 158
    Baked Beans, p 159
    Baked Corn on the Cob, p 164
    Cardamom Carrots, p 162
    Carrot Souffle, p 162
    Chinese Pickled Beets, p 160
    Corn Pie, p 165
    Corn Pudding, p 165
    Crumbly Green Beans, p 169
    Ginger Carrots, p 163
    Golden Parmesan Potatoes, p 171
    Gratin of Celery Root and Potato, p 163
    Greens with Garlic, Raisins & Pine Nuts, p 168
    Halushki, p 161
    Indian Rice, p 175
    Julienne Vegetable Saute, p 180
    Main Line Mashed Potatoes, p 171
    Moore Hash Browns, p 173
    Mushroom and Arugula Risotto, p 177
    Potato Filling, p 172
    Ratatouille, p 170
    Seasoned Onion Rice, p 175
    Spicy Sweet Broccoli, p 161
    Spinach Filled Tomatoes, p 178
    Stir-Fried Asparagus with Cashews, p 159
    Summer Squash Supreme, p 178
    Tomato Pudding, p 179
    Tomatoes and Zucchini Oriental, p 179
    Vegetable Couscous, p 174
    Zucchini Moussaka, p 181
Vegetarian Chili, p 63
Velvet Cheese Cake, p 247
Venison
    Hunter's Stew, p 125
    Mince Meat Pie, p 284
Versatile Cheese Strata, p 205
Vienna Bread, p 233

Waffles, p 215
Walnut
    Date Nut Cake, p 242
    Karithopeta, p 244
    Olive Nut Spread, p 18
    Pesto & Sun Dried Tomato Torte, p 21
War Cake, p 248
Wassail, p 45
Watercress
    Endive, Watercress & Pomegranate Salad, p 92
    Grilled Salmon with Watercress, p 145
    Watercress Sandwiches, p 34
White Chili, p 64
White Chocolate Fudge Cake, p 246
Whole Wheat Pancakes, p 214
Wild Rice Salad, p 86
Wilted Greens with Sweet and Sour Sauce, p 97
Worldly Beef Stroganoff, p 121

Your Own Wine, p 46

Zucchini
    Ratatouille, p 170
    Stuffed Cymlins with a Flavored Vinaigrette, p 96
    Tomatoes and Zucchini Oriental, p 179
    Zucchini Moussaka, p 181
    Zucchini Salad with Hot Bacon Dressing, p 95
Zuppa di Pesca, p 151

To Order More Cookbooks.......

Mail order to: Cumberland County Historical Society
21 North Pitt Street
Carlisle, Pennsylvania 17013
(717) 249-7610 Fax (717) 258-9332

Enclosed is my check for $39.00 which includes postage and handling. Pennsylvania residents add $2.10 sales tax (total $41.10). Please send a copy of *Past Receipts, Present Recipes* cookbook to:

Name_____

Address_____ Zip_____

City/State_____

✂--

Enclosed is my check for $39.00 which includes postage and handling. Pennsylvania residents add $2.10 sales tax (total $41.10). Please send a copy of *Past Receipts, Present Recipes* cookbook to:

Name_____

Address_____ Zip_____

City/State_____